Life Seeds and Codes

A MANUAL FOR BODY-MIND-SPIRIT
SYNERGY, BODY MINDFULNESS,
AND INTEGRATION

Brian T Roberts

AyniWrite Press
ALBUQUERQUE, NM

Copyright © 2021 by Brian T Roberts.

All rights reserved. No part of this publication may be reproduced, distributed, or transmitted in any form or by any means, including photocopying, recording, or other electronic or mechanical methods, without the prior written permission of the publisher, except in the case of brief quotations embodied in critical reviews and certain other noncommercial uses permitted by copyright law. For permission requests, write to the author at the address below.

Brian T Roberts
http://lifeseedcodes.com

Book Layout ©2013 BookDesignTemplates.com

Ordering Information:
All books available on Amazon.com

Life Seed Codes – A Manual for Body-Mind-Spirit Synergy, Body Mindfulness, and Integration / Brian T Roberts —1st ed.
ISBN 978-0-9984624-2-4

Dedication

Thank you to the following authors who contributed to this book: Richard Barrett, Seven Levels of Personal Consciousness, John Kanary, Seven Stages of Consciousness, Karin Couture, Thoughts on Hypnotherapy, Elmer Green, States of Consciousness, Edna Ballard, Praise Your Diamond Self, and Carole Conlon, LifeWeaving. These contributions have been generously donated by these individuals and greatly appreciated.

Contents

Author Preface ix
Author's Note & The Key Point xi
Introduction xiii
The Plan xv

PART ONE: THE BODY

Chapter 1 Introduction to The Body 3
Chapter 2 Background Information 5
  a. Alphabiotics 5
  b. B.E.S.T. 6
  c. Fight or Flight 7
  d. Balance is the Bottom Line 8
  e. How I Choose to Facilitate 9
Chapter 3 Brain Body Balancing Technique 11
  a. Definitions of the Elements to Get Started 11
  b. Administering the Pulse 13
  c. Balancing the Chakras 14
  d. The Pulse is Easy! 15
  e. Contraindications to Brain Body Balancing 17
  f. Wisdom of Knowing or Caring & Sharing 18
  g. Brain Body Balancing Used Together with Reiki 21
Chapter 4 Essays 27
  a. Morphogenic Fields The Hundredth Monkey 27
  b. On Getting Zapped 31
  c. The Chakras 35
  d. Words Energy Vibration 41
  e. The Seven Levels of Personal Consciousness 43

PART TWO: THE MIND

Chapter 5 Introduction to The Mind 49
Chapter 6 Essays 51
  a. Seven Principles of Hermetic Philosophy 51

- b. Cords 56
- c. On Brains and Minds 58
- d. About Sound 63
- e. Emotions 67
- f. Schumann Resonance 68
- g. Introduction to the Science of Huna 71
    - i. Yourself as the Trinity 74
    - ii. The Lower Self 74
    - iii. Prayer in Huna Philosophy 82
    - iv. The Sacred Trinity 84
    - v. Middle Self 85
    - vi. Superconscious Mind 87
    - vii. Cosmic Principles According to Huna 88
    - viii. Developing Personal Power 89
    - ix. The HA Rite Ritual 90
    - x. Ho'oponopono 93
- h. Thoughts on Hypnotherapy 104
- i. Why I Don't Tell People What to Do, What to Think or What to Believe 106
- j. Seven Stages of Consciousness 110

PART THREE: THE SPIRIT

Chapter 7 Introduction to The Spirit 117
Chapter 8 Essays on Spirit 119
- a. On Wisdom and Inspiration 119
- b. Our Evolution 120
- c. On Meditation 121
- d. Diamond Heart Energy Activations 123
- e. Praise Your Diamond Self 126
- f. Shaman's Creed/ Quantum Self/ Healer Oath 129
- g. Philosophy and Processes Go Like This 131
- h. Ascension 133
- i. First Religion, then Spirituality, then Mysticism and, now this, Letting Go and Letting God 136
- j. Hakomi – Body-Centered Psychotherapy, Diamond Heart Energy Activations, and a Little Personal History 138
- k. More on Hakomi 143
- l. Christianity and the Diamond Heart Energy 145

m.	The Law of Attraction	148
n.	States of Consciousness Diagram	152

PART FOUR: PROSE, POEMS AND ALMOST ZEN KOANS

Chapter 9 Introduction to Prose, Poems and Almost Zen Koans 165

- a. A Life Seed Code Poem 166
- b. Again and Again 168
- c. I AM 169
- d. Gazing into the Freedom Mirror 170
- e. Milestones and Gemstones 171
- f. Mystery and Silence 173
- g. When Gandhi Pours Your Tea 179
- h. Cycles 181
- i. Blessings 182
- j. Our Mothers 183
- k. Buddha and Nature 185
- l. Life Seed 186
- m. What Was Our Lady Doing When the Angel Came? 188
- n. Be Silent Then Sing 190
- o. Seeds to Sow 191
- p. Light Leads Life 193
- q. Freedom Mirror 196
- r. Silent Again 197
- s. See/ No Karma/ Eyes/ I 198
- t. I Believe 199
- u. The Key 200

Appendix 1: Affirmations 203
Appendix 2: Declaration of Light 204
Appendix 3: Reset Exercise 205
Appendix 4: Re-Set/Namaste Exercise 207
Appendix 5: Bija Seeds Mantra Meditation 208
Appendix 6: What DHEA is NOT 210
The Gifts 211
Author Bio 213

Go to Lifeseeds.com for updates on the Brain Body Balancing method

Author Preface

In a series of dreams, a chiropractor named Dr. Virgil Crane Sr., received the inspiration and technique that became key to Developmental Alphabiotics and the alignment process. He taught this process to his son Virgil Jr., who like his father became a chiropractor. Virgil Jr. realized shortly thereafter, that like Dorothy, he was simply not in Kansas anymore. He had crossed over the barrier from physical to metaphysical. He was doing something physical and getting highly spiritual results. *Also see YouTube presentations of Dr. Virgil Crane.*

By working to establish brain hemisphere integration, he was seeing not just neck, arms, backs, and legs getting better, and peoples' general health, but he saw whole people emerging from the shadow of stress, depression, anxiety, addiction, and often directionless, low vibration, confused and complicated realities. At this point, he was running a parallel course to the new thought, new age, and metaphysical movement. You might say in the highest of compliments that he was doing yoga on people.

He then decided to return his chiropractic license and founded The American Heritage Seminary. He began developing and teaching the Alphabiotic alignment process and began to ordain ministers and train them in what he now considered a sacrament. He felt that bringing a person into a state of balance was the greatest gift that one person could do for another.

I trained at Alphabiotic seminars in Dallas and with a local practitioner to get certified to practice. I practiced very diligently in Seattle for 10 years. Fast forward my life, fifteen years later, I responded to the need of an individual who was in great discomfort, having lost the normal use of her left arm. Her condition seemed complicated, so, initially I decided to do a bodywork session. She was very happy to receive some comfort. The next day she was off to see her chiropractor for a consultation. He had taken x-rays the week before, and the following day she sent a text saying that, in essence, she was a wreck and he wanted her in a program of three visits a week for six months. I returned a text telling her that I could teach her husband and children to do the Brain Body Balancing work. I recommended that she receive and participate in Diamond Heart Energy Activation so that we could align her body, mind, and spirit. The following day she came with her daughter and we had a session. After the session, she was 100 percent out of pain and had the full use of her left arm again. The following day I went to have dinner with her whole family and taught them the Pulse technique for Brain Body Balancing.

The moral of the story is that nature abhors a vacuum, the need was there, the willingness to share was present and now if this family will continue to do the balancing, we suspect that a harmony will prevail.

My last book came about in much the same way. *Be Clear Now* was an instructional book about dowsing, clearing and life, and we responded by organizing some beginner dowsing charts. They came beautifully into being and AyniWrite-Publishing offered to do the rest.

Presently I have two books on Amazon.com that contribute to this process, *I Am Presence the Diamond Heart Energy Activations*, and *Be Clear Now, a Beginners' Book for Pendulum Clearing*.

Service to Others vs. Service to Self

It is weird and wonderful how it rolls, when one is naturally in service to others in our great universe of possibilities. There is a profound synchronistic and organic nature to it when we merge with one another. Parts flow into wholes, movements with people, places and things form and flower, a harmony and flow are present. It all seems very natural, the sun rises, the wheels turn, you chop wood and carry water, fulfillment happens, and all things return to the One. This is the way that nature intended things to be. This is the turning of the wheel of dharma. Yes, it does happen sometimes.

The purpose of this exercise is to get you and your loved ones back to a beautiful state of balance and to stay there, to thrive and be alive.

It has been said that the greatest gift one person can do for another is to bring them out of the shadows of stress, of fight or flight and to bring them into a state of balance.

Here are the tools to do just that:

> The capacity to self-correct, to self-regulate, to self-heal is a quality that is consistent in all living systems, but first the body must be released from harmful fight or flight patterns.

So let's do this thing.

Author's Note and the Key Point

It's All About the Asking

The Diamond Heart Energy Activations with the 12-guided meditations went on Amazon Books a few years back. The title for this work is *I AM Presence Diamond Heart Energy Activations,* consisting of a handbook with 12-guided meditations with music and guitar, cello and bass. I play the guitar and sing the Moola mantra. I still do activations most every day. A client asked me to record the activations for her and although I thought at first that it would not be as effective, we soon found it very powerful. Being a bodyworker and brain body balancer for so many years, having the recorded sessions freed me up to do the hands-on healing, energy work and balancing with the sessions.

The key point is that a client asked.

My next book or manual was called *Be Clear Now*, an introduction to pendulum dowsing and clearing. This exercise was born out of a need to share the clearing work with our friend Judy whose daughter was struggling with her energy. At first, I thought that it could be an addendum to the first book, but my publisher suggested we do another book. I am so delighted to have accomplished and completed the task.

Not long ago, I did a remote energy session for a gal in Columbia and she reported back that she was feeling better, sleeping better and being better. The Lord moves in mysterious ways. His or her angels do great long distance work.

A few weeks back a friend in need became a friend indeed when I entered in on behalf of her wellbeing. A car accident had left her severely compromised. She could barely raise her left arm and had lived with much pain for over seven years. Given that she lives a four-hour drive from me I offered to train her family in the brain body balancing, chakra balancing and hands on healing process. She is now doing really well right now and we aim to keep her this way. She is an amazing artist. One of my favorite things to do now is to receive a session and get my own energy fine-tuned. My partner Karin is really quite proficient at the work. In fact, she is right behind me working on her two daughters I love how the universe is moving us right now. It is great to respond to our cosmic family and watch our creative abilities open and flow, benefiting each other along the way. Also, my friend, publisher, and dowsing teacher

Carole Conlon has been a total miracle worker in every way, including multi-dimensionally.

Again, the key point is that all of the material has come into being as a direct result from requests from clients, friends and family. In other words, people "ASK" and then the downloads come in multiple forms. Some say we live in a universe of Ask, Seek and Knock and it is opened to us.

This book, *Life Seeds and Codes,* gives me the opportunity to share essays with clients in my healing arts practice. Sometimes one simple essay goes a long way. Also, I think being prepared sometimes is better than having a plan. Where having a plan can cause God to laugh, while having preparedness allows for spontaneity, participation, and wonder.

Introduction

A Manual for Body Mind Spirit Synergy
Body Mindfulness and Integration.

This manual has been in development for over four decades. Of course, I had no idea at any time in the past that I might arrive at this point and be beginning to energize the main ingredients of the Diamond Heart Energy Activations, beginner's dowsing, Bodywork and Brain Body Balancing, FloMotion movement awareness and sensory biofeedback. Here we have lots of tools that are my pleasure to share with friends and travelers on the path of wholeness. The first two books on Amazon books came as direct requests by clients to make available the activations and the dowsing charts. This trilogy of body-mind-spirit unfolded really all together.

There are three sections in the manual: Section One is on the Body and offers Brain Body Balancing instruction and Flo Motion Movement Awareness. The instructional DVD Flomotion is available FREE as a digital download. It is called the 'Slow Motion Guide to Flow Motion' and is a wonderful presentation of each of the basic movements with original music by Brian. The device I called the Flo has a new name of the "liquid trainer" available at www.LiquidTrainer.com. There are also instructions for the Brain Body technique. These essays herein are very helpful for clients at the spas that I work at. They assist the receptionists when describing styles and methods to clients and are also practical to the students who are coming forward to train in the methods.

All participation is a voluntary action and unfolds with each individual, in his or her own order and development. You can use one of the tools, some of the tools, or all the tools. You can start wherever you wish and go, in any direction and timing that you wish. You are your own laboratory living in the body-mind-spirit-trinity/unity here on earth and doing what it is you came to do, hopefully. I offer facilitation, which is very different from teaching. Most all the tools, techniques in our methods can only unfold out of our own focused attention, effort, and grace. Sometimes, I will give a participant homework, but I will never check it, never. All good things flow from above downwards and from inside out. Each tool and technique are offered freely, and each individual is free to apply and pass on as they see fit.

Life is better in balance. Brain Hemisphere synchronization is now possible thanks to the pioneering work of many Chiropractic doctors and in my ability to crack the code and make this technique and discipline available to folks, friends, and family. I practiced it for 10 years and saw the breakthroughs that people have with a "life in balance." I have trained either directly or indirectly with many doctors and my approach to bodywork has been organized around the idea of interfacing the body for deep therapeutic results. My orientation is now shifting to do more mindfulness, relaxation, and meditation styles of bodywork where I borrow more from the Trager method and FloDynamics, speaking to the body to encourage deep release and body mind integrity. I will always Brain Body Balance people whenever I have someone on a table. Always. My use of Acupressure, Cross Fiber and Trager style or Flo-dynamics varies from session to session. I need to mention that I have been working with the Flo Motion Movement Awareness system for over thirty years. The sensory aspect of Flo is discovered, developed, and utilized by making a point to work, play and apply one's discoveries learned by doing the movements.

I am calling this third book or method book the one that will never be finished because I plan to keep putting up essays for free download on the web site. I will also keep inviting others to do the same. There are already many wonderful contributors to this manual. Together we can learn about the synergy of body-mind-spirit and make our discoveries available to one another.

When I offer a Brain Body Balancing technique tutorial, I like to do the Diamond Heart Energy Activation # 1, and work with Karin Couture, my partner. We do what we call a four-hands session. I also like to make myself available to bodyworkers and instruct them in the mechanics of the work wherever I am at the time. It is good to be flexible, so welcome to the play, work, training and development with the Life Seeds and Codes, and may your journey be rich with personal discovery, and empowered with tools to assist yourself and others.

Feel free to jump into any section and read any essay, as this is a circular study method with each part empowering the whole.

The Plan

To Teach, to Train, to Inspire and to Illuminate

The plan is to intrude upon the mood of mediocrity of a culture struggling with very closed systems of thought, too much control, too bizarre a distribution of wealth, challenges and attacks on our health and well-being, Wall Street bankers, and the culture of the military industrial complex, and earth changes.

The war on all fronts can only be avoided by a deep peace within and a great and fluid ability to keep on keeping on, which often includes changing directions. The master plan is to bring in more "light" slowly, patiently, and compassionately for the body, mind, and spirit.

Body - Brain Balancing and Beyond

Mind - Meditation Initiation and Be Clear Now

Spirit - I Am Presence, Diamond Heart Energy Activations and further Source related downloads and inspirations

Note: The books are all available on Amazon.com or available directly from Brian at http://lifeseedcodes.com

For myself this has been unfolding for over 40 years. I was fortunate to have been a student at the Ma Yoga Shakti Ashram in Deerfield Beach, Florida in 1972. Here I was exposed to so many people from around the New Age movement, teachers and visiting Yogi's from India, channels and bodyworkers like senior Rolfer John Lodge, Hoshino Therapy, Postural Integration. This then launched me into a lifelong study of the healing arts. The whole idea is to stay with the present, move with the Tao of things, and keep and stay interested, focused, and moving forward. To achieve and maintain a state of balance is a rare and beautiful thing. It is available and it is natural, and some people can and will do this.

When our personal alchemical fires run hot, the challenges of our lives help us develop character and bring us to a greater sense of mastery. This is a journey in higher consciousness. It is, while being an exercise in self-inquiry and self-examination, a true "service to others" process. Our being present and balanced is sort of mandatory. One does not have to spend years of time and thousands of dollars to begin. You may have been empowered to learn the Brain Body Balancing from a friend and now are seeing what it may have in store for you at deeper levels. You are welcome to come and go as you please. Take a piece and see how it fits presently into your own collage of tools, techniques, and experimentations'.

Having channeled the Diamond Heart Energy Activations from my own I AM Presence; I continue to do the activations daily for the benefit of my outer self or personality. The energy that is downloaded daily infuses the light most significantly, and that is every day.

For the body, we have a time-tested process for Brain Body Balancing and for synchronizing the brain hemispheres. This hands-on process also involves working in the subtle circuitry of the body, grounding the body through the Omega Point, and balancing the chakras. For the mind domain, we have the I AM meditation and the mantras, Bija mantras for meditation and the Moola Mantra for chanting or listening. For the spirit we have the Diamond Heart Energy Activations on 12-guided recorded programs, plus the I AM workbook. These are not belief systems, but rather a Be/Lived program for balance, for harmony, for self-development. In Section Two of this book, we will be introduced to the philosophy of Huna. In Section Three, we will take a peek at Hakomi work.

All these tools and techniques work with the I AM Presence to recalibrate and make subtle energy adjustments that keep us fluid and more flexible, upgraded and more able to make or move through the shifts that are upon us as the planet itself goes through its ascension process. The Ankh was a symbol used in the church of Ageless Wisdom where I studied in the seminary, and then was ordained as a minister. The director of our church was a trance medium that channeled a woman being named Fay Uh Tay Una from Venus. This goddess-like being was truly the head of our church. What a powerful demonstration of love, of service and dedication I observed in my associations with them.

Our model is a unity model. All are welcome to join in. All creeds, all races, all sizes, and all colors at any level of spiritual enfoldment are welcome to begin, to learn, to embrace and to share. It would please me so that you would learn to do the brain balancing and teach others.

Be a channel for light and frequency, trust the force. I was once introduced to a woman in Aspen, Colorado and I shook hands with her. About a half hour later she came over to me and asked me what I did. She told me that her hand was bothering her all day and suddenly was better. Healing happens, Unity happens, Oneness happens. The more you work in mindfulness with your own I AM Presence <u>in whatever form is appropriate to you</u> and focus your intention, invoke the colors for the chakras for healing and transformation, the quicker YOU WILL BECOME "a universal oscillating frequency instrument." The more you work with the process, principles, ideas, and energies the quicker you own it. It is all about time in Source energy or as they say in running the energy.

When you made a commitment, Courage
Becomes available to you.

When you have opened in Compassion, Strength
Becomes available to you.

When you have let go in humility, the Power of the Universe
Becomes available to you.

When you stand in your Truth, mindfully,
The universe flows through you.

PART ONE

BODY

PART ONE

BODY

CHAPTER 1

Introduction to The Body

There are certain things that only trained persons should attempt to do.
There are simple things that almost anyone can do.
The wisdom lies in knowing the difference.
This is simple and you can do it!

It is very easy to purchase a massage table and to learn this Alpha Brain & Body Balancing technique, and teach someone else, friend, family, husband, wife, and/or children, etc.; to exchange this process. Try Craigslist or offer-up where you can purchase a massage table sometimes for less the $50 in your local area. We recently purchased three tables for a total of $215; the retail value on these would have been at least $1,500.

That being said, this technique that was developed by many different contributing practitioners, is being given out at this time in great hopes that many persons will see the wisdom in doing and receiving the process. You might say, service to others type of people should be quick to recognize, utilize and appreciate the gift.

The fight or flight mechanism is designed by nature and the body to protect us. If you have ever had to swerve your car or suddenly hit the brakes, you will notice that things slow down.

Your brain drops out of sync into a lower level brain function during any emergency. This is designed to protect you. The trouble is that people have to hit the brakes all the time in some part of their lives. What may also surprise you is that the same effect is happening a lot of the time while you are watching suspenseful movies.

Normally, the brain function returns to normal except if you are in your car and you have another half an hour to drive, it is going to extend that fight or flight mechanism. The cause of so many extensions is keeping people stuck in the fight or flight state.

Any time of day, if you were to set up a table, say at a mall and test 100 people through muscle testing you would discover that at least 90 percent of the people would be stuck in an inappropriate stress pattern with the wisdom of the body being misdirected.

In the times that we live in, it is normal to be locked in an inappropriate stress state. It is just not natural. So the process here is laid out in the hands-on method in this section to refresh your memory.

Up next, The Hands-On Method of the Alpha Brain Body Balancing...

CHAPTER 2

Background Information

Alphabiotics

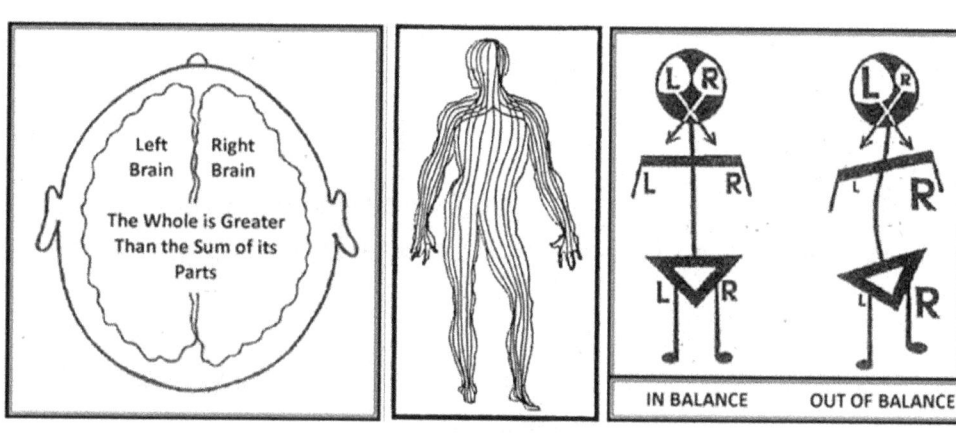

An Alphabiotic Alignment is a hands-on process that acts as a catalyst, a way of flipping on a switch so to speak, to a higher level of right-brain/left-brain synchronicity. When successful, one's subtle vibratory life energies, or Spirit, come into a fuller, more glorious expression in the mind-body allowing for seemingly miraculous shifts on all planes . . . and at every level of your being. It can bring you back into harmony with your Divine Essence. The alignment is a facilitation. It frees the innate power, inherent within the mind-body. This renewing essence, when liberated, radiates through one's being, dissolving instances of physical and mental malaise as light obliterates darkness. Properly utilized, a very real shift in consciousness can blossom. As we spend sustained time in this new realm of higher brain integration, our entire cellular being, as well as our reality, (re)-organizes and attunes around the vibratory frequency of new, more positive, and loving thought forms. Being elemental to its integrity, the new frequency stimuli assist to reinstate our original blueprint. It is this core level phenomenon that is believed to be responsible for the transformation of life experience so often realized.

Benefits of a Balanced Brain

The two hemispheres of the brain, one creative and one analytical, are connected by a bundle of nerves. Once we handle a crisis, the body should return to its normal state between those two sections. However, what happens today is that we go into a stress state and lock up, so the body believes it needs to be prepared to fend off attack most of the time, perpetual stress.

Negativity also builds up when the brain's hemispheres are not communicating well. The negative words we hear all day long and negative emotions that bombard us affect our emotional bodies. Stress gets worse.

An Alphabiotic alignment, called a lift, unifies the brain hemispheres, and opens you up to alpha brainwave states, which allow access to the entire brain. Now you can draw from your natural and God-given talents to co-create with life; your innate wisdom is able to guide the processes of the body, such as healing and metabolism.

Once released from its inappropriate stress pattern and balance is achieved, the innate wisdom of the body is freed up to direct healing in the area which most needs it, while at the same time, you experience greater clarity and life vision.

> Excerpts reprinted with permission from portions of an article by Winifred O'Brien,
> *The New Times*, Feb. 1994, Vol.9, No.9.

For more information about Alphabiotics check out
www.alphabioticsonline.com/

B.E.S.T.
More on Brain Hemisphere Synchronization

The patients that were involved in a B.E.S.T. study had failed to respond to other medical care and other forms of chiropractic treatments. They were required to have been in chiropractic care for a minimum of six months. Researchers felt if they saw a 15% improvement in the casework, the utilization of B.E.S.T. (Bio-Energetic-

Synchronization-Technique) would be considered clinically significant. Overwhelmingly successful, the results provided an 85% improvement in the patients, not only in their areas of primary pain, but in other areas of their lives such as improved emotional stress level and overall well-being.

The Bio-energetic Synchronization Technique, like the Alphabiotic Unification Process, works with brain hemisphere synchronization as its focus. The techniques are very different, but the results are quite similar. Brain Body Balancing is a simple method derived from chiropractic principal, but because of its simplicity and gentleness, it may be utilized by all health care practitioners.

Fight or Flight

The fight or flight response is our body's primal, automatic, inborn response that prepares the body to "fight" or "take flight" when there is any sense of danger coming from the environment. It is our survival mechanism. This can be triggered from internal or external circumstances.

When our fight or flight response is activated, sequences of nerve cell firing occur and chemicals like adrenaline, noradrenalin and cortisol are released into our bloodstream. There are plenty of other changes that occur to our physiology such as increased breathing rate, blood moves away from our internal organs out to the muscles, which require more fuel for action, awareness intensifies, and pupils may dilate as vision sharpens, impulses quicken. It can be a lot like driving a car while keeping the other foot slightly pressed on the brakes. We spin our wheels if there is not a "real" threat. Guess what? Most of the times there is not. As a lifeguard in Florida, I experienced a few times the need for speed and accuracy. I was pumped and got results in a few rescue missions. Driving up and down the interstate is a whole other story. I don't really need the pumping action of the muscles, but it can happen anyway if you are forced to hit the brakes.

It may be that our world today, with our aggressive, hypervigilant, and over-reactive participants, is actually moving further away from the desired outcomes of peace, personal power and prosperity. Of course, the hormones that are required to run the stress program also have a seriously negative impact on the body/mind, the immune system, our emotional life, and our endocrine system. Your body could be making DHEA, which keeps us young, but if misdirected by the survival instinct, fight or flight, it is making cortisol and messing with your blood sugars.

There is something very profound about our body's abilities to protect itself. The ability to move from the higher levels of brain function down into the lower levels and returning again to the higher levels, is the magic of a highly evolved biological system. *The problem is if we do drop down into a lower level of the brain and lateralize into one brain hemisphere, we should be able to come out normally and naturally within 20 minutes. This is not what is happening!!!!!*

Point of fact, we are simply not returning to balance due to the rapid rate of our lives, the stresses of the modern world, physical, mental, emotional, and energetic. We are dealing with electromagnetic toxicity in the form of cell phones, cell towers, power lines and stations, smart meters on our homes and businesses, and on and on. By the time a person drives to work, deals with a toxic work environment, sits in a dead building with poor ventilation, sitting next to a computer and then drives home again, they are lucky to make it alive. If possible, after all your driving is done, the very best time for you to get worked on is right at that moment.

The capacity to self-correct to self-heal to self-regenerate is a quality of all living systems, but this can only happen in a state of homeostasis, or balance. A whole person consists of a variety of parts that comprise the whole. When functioning from the whole brain you have a greater possibility of functioning as a healthy whole person.

Balance is the Bottom Line

A gift that could keep on giving: A life in balance will absolutely result in greater satisfaction, growth, evolution, creativity and achievement.

> *"Necessity is the mother of invention."*   Anonymous

> *"There are things that only highly skilled persons can facilitate.*
> *There are simple things that anyone can and probably should do.*
> *Wisdom lies in understanding the difference."*
> Brian T Roberts

How I Choose to Facilitate

The reason why our culture can produce so many incredible athletes, like basketball players, for instance, is because every schoolyard in America has a basketball hoop.

NOTE: We ask everyone that is trained in this healing method to share "The Pulse and Alpha Brain Body Balancing" with at least one other person. We are hoping that the timing is right for a wave like this.

The myth of the expert falls flat on its face right here. No more elitism, no more experts, no more Dr Moe, Dr Larry, Dr Curley, no more depriving others, and ourselves of a simple sense of balance. No more three times a week for six months of driving to an office to be a number.

Remember I said, "There are simple things that anyone can and probably should do."

To our senses it appears that the sun revolves around the earth. We know this is not correct. The conspiracy of the senses goes on to influence many of our misconceptions. Life is short! The older you become you would think the longer life would seem, become, or feel. No such thing.

The body, the coil, has become our identity and limits our supersensory development. If we do not push consciously into the subtle energy, the field, the breath, the chakras, mindfulness, and the spirit, we will be too identified with the physical body alone and bound by a sense of false security, by false concept and by a lack of realization of the true and of the truth. The "I AM Presence" fails to be a fact in life and for many that might be considered sacred, like our lives, is nothing but trouble. This is not the divine plan. My heart tells me otherwise.

People who see the wisdom in balance, who can reach out with kindness, care, and compassion, or even just curiosity, will see some of the results that accompany mindfulness and balance.

I practiced Alphabiotic work in Seattle for 10 years and saw amazing healing events happen. The method, which works with brain hemisphere integration, is an amazing process, but the thrust technique it employs can be a bit rough. Alpha Brain Body Balancing by comparison is so very gentle, and it synchronizes the left and right hemispheres of the brain. Every hand's on health care provider would do well to learn it, experience it, apply it, but most of all, lay people can learn to use it with friends and family and participate in the giving and receiving of positive and healing energy.

I call Alpha Brain Body Balancing a 'science for the Golden Age' because I can appreciate that when we all come up and out from a lower level of brain function (reptilian), when we stop out-picturing "fight or flight," when control and dominance over one another has been superseded by a sense of co-operation, collaboration and unity, there will be whole people functioning out of the neo-cortex, whole brain and Source connected. People at a higher level seek unity, collaboration, equanimity, and peace. Let's get there! Let's stay there! Let's be what the Creator provided for us, for ourselves, for our creativity and freedom, and for one another.

Let's do this thing! Let's do it right. Let's do it better this time. Let's begin to facilitate a wave of people to "extend a sense of balance" to one another across the country and the world.

Oh, and by the way, no one said you had to limit yourself to one person. Feel free to train everyone who will learn it.

CHAPTER 3

Brain Body Balancing Technique

We recently encountered a woman who had just returned from Florida and was exposed to the energy of Hurricane Irma. She was still quite rattled. After the first tune-up she said that she felt taller. After the fourth day, she said that <u>she felt like herself again</u>. That was the greatest compliment we could have ever received.

Alpha Brain Body Balancing
Definition of the Elements to Get Started

Grounding, Visualizing, Mapping, Tapping, Clearing, Balancing and Synchronizing Terminology

Grounding and Visualizing: Beginning on the Omega Point (located on the soles of the feet), visualize golden cords attached to the bottom of your feet and flowing into the healing temple at the center of the earth/into Gaia.

Declaration of Intent: Tell Gaia (Mother Earth) that you want to match frequencies for the benefit of health, of yourself and of your client. The goal is matching your frequencies to the ever shifting and ascending frequencies of the planet.

Mapping: Our touch with hands, palms, and fingers fully attached to the body allow a person to simply become more aware of his or her physical body, by inviting increased sensory awareness to the area. Touch tells a story. Let's make it as beautiful as possible.

Tapping: Very light touch is sufficient for all tapping on the head and the sternum. It might be considered a flow of electrical energy that is moving out of the hands of the practitioner, about 50%:50% mechanical to electrical. By alternating tapping with mapping, we are communicating with the innate wisdom of the body to address any imbalances of the body/mind. Congestion, muscle memory, and emotions are released, and a redirection of the innate wisdom occurs.

Clearing: People consist of electromagnetic energies that often are in exchange with their environments, people, places, and things. People often get energetic cords attached to them and often pick up energetic disturbances that cling-on. When we are clearing and balancing a chakra, we visualize a color and set the intention that any of these attachments (disturbances) are eliminated (neutralized, deconstructed). Only the clear light of the chakra remains.

Balancing: Balancing is a broad term that we utilize understanding that it is the body's own wisdom to maintain. By using the circle symbol with the vertical and horizontal sweep, and having the intention of extending our balance, the result is a return to what is normal and natural and balanced.

Synchronization (The Pulse): On the cranium is the key to the process. By moving the cranium gently, but rapidly, we send a signal by moving the brain inside the cranium. This causes the brain, a sensory response mechanism to re-set to a higher brain function. The desired and normal flow of information can now re-establish itself through the bridge called the corpus callosum. Having access to the neocortex (the highest level of the brain) is not just optimal, it is necessary for our healing, wellness, creativity, balance, and ascension. Persons who have access to the whole brain or the neocortex have their attention focused in the present. Be here now, be clear now, being in sync now is where you want to be.

A Sensory Response Mechanism: The brain is not attached to the inside of the cranium by muscles or connective tissue but, more or less, sits in the cranial fluids. Any gentle tap is going to stimulate the neocortex or seventh levels of the brain and allow the nervous system to re-set, synchronize and balance. We turn off the stresses and turn on the power of the body. The result is harmony.

If you like, you can listen to the "I AM Presence" meditation before entering into the balancing. You can play this during your session. If you wish to do a full session, which takes 12 minutes with the meditation, you can find it for FREE at http://Lifeseedcodes.com. Other options are to use meditation/relaxing music from any source desirable.

Alpha Brain Body Balancing
Administering the Pulse

*Audio instruction of this process is available for your benefit.
Contact Karin at karilou444@gmail.com*

Use essential oils when available. A couple of drops of Valor from Young Living Oil is a perfect start. If you are already working with essential oils, and working with intention and visualization, just add music and you will be incorporating four unique elements together to bring about a shift, an upgrade, and a balancing.

STEP #1—

1st Hand Position: Have your participant lie face down on the massage table, place your thumbs on the Omega points (on the left and right feet, 2 inches above the big toe and at the mid-line of the foot.)

Visualize a golden cord coming out of the bottom of your feet and going into the center of the earth. Hold both points for 20 seconds.

STEP #2—

2nd Hand Position: Place your left hand over the back of the left knee, place your right hand at the base of the right ankle area. Hold for 20 seconds.

Reverse hands for next position by placing your right hand on the right knee and the left hand at the base of the left ankle area. Hold for 20 seconds.

STEP #3—

3rd hand position. Place your left hand on the left knee and the right hand on the right hip. Hold for 20 seconds.

Reverse hands for next position by placing the right hand on the right knee and the left hand on the left hip. Hold for 20 seconds.

STEP #4—

4th hand position. Place your left hand on the left shoulder, right hand on the right hip. Hold for 20 seconds.

Reverse hands for next position by placing the right hand on the right shoulder and the left hand on left hip. Hold for 20 seconds. (You can use whatever hand is comfortable for placing on the shoulder and hip.)

Alpha Brain Body Balancing
Balancing the Chakras

1st Chakra (Root /Instinctual/Survival Chakra)   Red

Visualize the color red, hold your hand over the chakra for 10 seconds, then slowly make a circle counterclockwise, move the hand vertically then horizontally to make a cross in the center of the circle. Next, slowly inscribe a circle in a clockwise motion, and again move the hand vertically then horizontally to make another cross in the center of that circle. Minimum time over area is 20 seconds. There is no problem in going longer if you so desire.

2nd Chakra (Creativity/Sex Chakra)   Orange

Visualize the color orange, hold your hand over the chakra for 10 seconds, then slowly make a circle counterclockwise, move the hand vertically then horizontally to make a cross in the center of the circle. Next, slowly inscribe a circle in the clockwise motion, and again move the hand vertically then horizontally to make another cross in the center of that circle.

3rd Chakra (Solar Plexus/power chakra)   Yellow

Visualize the color yellow, hold your hand over the chakra for 10 seconds, then slowly make a circle counterclockwise, move the hand vertically then horizontally to make a cross in the center of the circle. Next, slowly inscribe a circle in the clockwise motion, and again move the hand vertically then horizontally to make another cross in the center of that circle.

4th Chakra (Heart /Love and Grace Chakra)   Green

Visualize the color green, hold your hand over the chakra for 10 seconds, then slowly make a circle counterclockwise, move the hand vertically then horizontally to make a cross in the center of the circle. Next, slowly inscribe a circle in the clockwise motion, and again move the hand vertically then horizontally to make another cross in the center of that circle.

5th Chakra (Throat/Communication/Truth Chakra) — Blue

Visualize the color blue, hold your hand over the chakra for 10 seconds, then slowly make a circle counterclockwise, move the hand vertically then horizontally to make a cross in the center of the circle. Next, slowly inscribe a circle in the clockwise motion, and again move the hand vertically then horizontally to make another cross in the center of that circle.

6th Chakra (3rd Eye/Seeing is Believing Chakra) — Indigo

Visualize the color indigo, hold your hand over the chakra for 10 seconds, then slowly make a circle counterclockwise, move the hand vertically then horizontally to make a cross in the center of the circle. Next, slowly inscribe a circle in the clockwise motion, and again move the hand vertically then horizontally to make another cross in the center of that circle.

7th Chakra (Crown/Unity Chakra) — White/Gold

Visualize the color white/gold, hold your hand over the chakra for 10 seconds, then slowly make a circle counterclockwise, move the hand vertically then horizontally to make a cross in the center of the circle. Next, slowly inscribe a circle in the clockwise motion, and again move the hand vertically then horizontally to make another cross in the center of that circle.

Alpha Brain Body Balancing
The Pulse is Easy!

When you are pulsing, imagine that you are sending a wave of energy up from the earth through your whole body affecting the persons total energy field.

<u>IMPORTANT: Never pulse anybody without padding for the head</u>. The pulse should only be administered while utilizing the proper headrest, such as a massage table, body contour pillow or neck cushion.

The Pulse Technique

Method #1: The Recipient is Face Down on the Table

1. Stand on the left side of the table by the head of your subject, lying face down on the table.

2. Place your index and middle fingers on the left side of the cranium at the base of the head (lower lobe).
3. "Pulse" one time by pushing down and away diagonally towards the right front eye. Imagine a vector moving from back left to front right. The amount of pressure is equal to the force required to "break an egg" without breaking the yoke.
4. If you have time, allow each person to rest for 20 to 30 seconds after the "Pulse" and then begin working the chakras from the bottom up from the right side of the table and then "Pulse" again.
5. Let the person rest/relax for 30 seconds (minimum) while their body integrates that dynamic energy suggestion.
6. The first highest option is to repeat the whole process, but now stand on the right side of the person and starting again from the Omega point, through the body, do all the chakras and the pulse. (This repeat process is not required, but it allows for a longer session promoting more relaxation, integration, body-mapping, and healing to occur).

The second highest option is re-do the seven chakras and the pulse, from the right side. (The pulse is now done on the right side of the head.)

The third highest option is to just do the pulse on the right side of the head. Always pulse both sides of the head and remember to pause a minimum of 30 seconds between the left and right pulse.

I have trained people who I think "pulse" too hard and others who "pulse" too light. However, the result is the same. It works every time.

I tend to work on the left side first. The left side represents the feminine and receptive side.

Method#2: Recipient is Face Up on the Table

This option offers a longer session or is good for any person who cannot rest on the front of his or her body; you can offer a face up energy balancing:

1. Have your person lie face up on the table. *NOTE: If you have just done the face down aspect and pulsed them, wait 15 seconds and contact the omega chakra for 15 seconds. If not start with Step #2.*
2. Begin with 10 to 15 seconds of tapping on the head. Make sure your hand is open and makes contact with both sides of the brain hemispheres.
3. Activate the omega point for 10 to 15 seconds.

1. Place hands on left ankle and right knee for 10 to 15 seconds. Switch hands to right ankle and left knee for 10 to 15 seconds.
2. Place hands on left knee and right hip for 10 to 15 seconds. Switch to hands on right knee and left hip for 10 to 15 seconds.
3. Tap lightly on the sternum for 10 to 15 seconds.
4. Place hands on left hip and right shoulder for 10 to 15 seconds. Place hands on right hip and left shoulder for 10 to 15 seconds.
5. Tap on the head for 10 to 15 seconds.
6. Ground at the omega point.

Stay open to your intuition and repeat any steps if you feel so guided.

For access to the instruction video, contact Brian at lifeseed108@hotmail.com
Music suggestion: *Ambience* by Robert Aviles

Contraindications to Brain Body Balancing

This is first and foremost a wellness strategy, gentle enough for a four-year-old; gentle enough for an eighty-four-year-old. The ideas presented are for the emerging culture of mindful and practical self-help and self-development enthusiasts. It is a very simple, very gentle and very dynamic process. When administered properly on a professional massage table with a good quality foam headrest, there should *never* be any possibility of injury. The foam support for the face and head is more than sufficient to absorb the small amount of pressure that is applied to the back of the head during the "Pulse." Remember to start gently with the "Pulse" and as you develop you will notice more ease and fluidity with the movement.

Things to be aware of when doing Alpha Brain Body Balancing
- See your doctor if you are having symptoms of any kind. The technique outlined in this book for the hands-on work of Alpha Brain Body Balancing is NOT INTENDED to be a substitute for medical or chiropractic care.
- Do NOT Participate if you, the practitioner, are having any structural, neck pain or headache symptoms.
- The one constant is the importance of using a FOAM headrest. <u>Never pulse anybody without padding for the head.</u>

- The best option when doing the pulse is to use a massage table with a head-rest.
  Option #2. A Body Contour Pillow with the headrest available from: www.BodySupport.com. This seems to work very well when placed on a bed, couch, or sofa.
  #3 Option would be to get a thick circular neck pillow that many people use when flying. These pillows are available everywhere, the thicker the better. If you do use this make sure you are on a bed or a couch or sofa.
- DO NOT WORK ON THE FLOOR.

Wisdom of Knowing, or Caring and Sharing

When I train a person to do the "Pulse," I ask them to please facilitate at least one other person.

This means I want them (or you) to train somebody! This then immediately places us on the same level or playing field. The myth of the expert is not supported here. After all, it is the wisdom of the body that heals the body. We are not doing so much as we are undoing anyway. We are undoing the effects of gravity and modern living. The Course in Miracles states in Principle #9 that:

> *"Miracles are a kind of exchange. Like all expressions of Love, which are always miraculous in the true sense, the exchange reverses the physical laws. They bring more love to both the giver and the receiver."*

They are saying here that Higher Energy, Love or let us say Quantum Energy is working in a different way. It is not new energy; we just recently put our attention on it. If I give you my watch, I lose it. If I tell you what time it is, we both have this information, no energy loss. If we want to expand the conversation towards the idea of unity or the collective human energy field, I could say that every time you or someone trained as a result of this effort balances another, it lifts the human spirit and increases us all. We are participating in a collective field of energy, of consciousness. It has a great influence on how and when we enter into an age of peace, an age of light, and the golden age. This matters to everyone whether they are conscious of this or not. Let's choose love! Let's choose to take some of the burden off the world soul and move collectively into the light.

Lately, the more I find myself in service to others, the more the miracles are unfolding. My first book and the 12-guided meditations accompanying them, came into being as a result of a request from a participant. I was not convinced it would work and then we recorded it and were pleasantly surprised. The Diamond Heart Energy Activations CD's happened and then Carole Conlon of AyniWrite Press offered to put the book on Amazon. The second book *Be Clear Now - A Beginners Guide to Pendulum Clearing,* was the result of simplifying the charts for a friend. It began simply and ended elegantly. This effort was born out of necessity, as I cannot offer the work to friends and family that are distributed now all over the country. Now we have other options.

The "Pulse" is a key to whole brain function, to healing and wholeness, everybody can benefit from this, and it is time to create a wave of energy and higher vibration. One that has energy and vitality within it to shift us towards the higher dimensions of light; so please volunteer to be a giver and a receiver. Together we can put planetary bad karma in reverse and move in the spirit of collaboration, one person at a time. Join in and bring your family and your friends. We can hardly go anywhere without our massage table, body contour pillows, or neck pillows so we can facilitate one another.

Each and every person and each and every time a person enters into this state of wholeness, they enter into new and expanded dynamic possibility. They up regulate themselves and place themselves in natural healing possibility patterns. The body regenerates on a 12 to 1 ratio. A person with a chronic health disorder for 12 years needs to be kept in balance for a year for the body to heal itself. There are other conditions such as stuttering which I have personally observed dynamically reversing. I have observed persons with vision improvement. A woman once came in to see if she could be assisted for a TMJ (temporal mandibular joint) inflammation and after a few weeks of balancing, hearing was restored in her left ear. My participant who had stuttered for 14 years was completely restored. The wisdom of the body corrected this problem for him.

There is obviously a physical aspect of the "Pulse," but the intention is always metaphysical, quantum and spiritual. We wish to express our gratitude to the professionals who have dedicated their lives to helping us facilitate this work. We appreciate those folks who manufacture our massage tables, body pillows, etc. Now like Reiki, Kofutu, and the many systems of energy work, the "Pulse" is ready to be uploaded into the collective field to be integrated into each person's tool kit for healing and transformation. There is a saying that if the only tool one has in their toolbox is a hammer, every problem looks like a nail. It is my opinion that there is a broad application to the "Pulse" Brain/Body Balancing.

When a person is in a stress-state and brain is lateralized, there is strength of the body on one side, weakness on the other. If a person is competing in any sports or physical competition, in balance they will lift more, run faster and sharpen all skills such as focus, rhythm, timing, aim and execution. It is pure and simple, and it works every time. I was once training a client in the Flo-Motion Movement System and he was having serious coordination challenges. I decided to have him lie down on a table at the gym. I brain balanced him and when he got up, he immediately was able to execute the movements. He was shocked and amazed. He was delighted and it was a pleasure to see, for both of us.

They say that it is easier to find a unicorn than it is to find a person in balance. Nowadays, I am finding children as young as four and five years old that are out of balance. Children gravitate towards these sessions. They request it from me.

I know a family that lives on a farm, eats all organic food, and takes the best care of their kids and, you know what, often the kids test out of balance. When I measure the leg length it is obvious that one leg is longer than the other leg (I'll explain this in detail later), indicating that one hemisphere is sending more energy and access to the neo-cortex and is compromised. I generally just do a short session of chakra balancing and then "Pulse" with children and they love it. As a parent with young children, wouldn't you want to take a few minutes a couple of times a week to balance these gentle guys and girls? Musicians would never perform without first tuning their instruments.

There is an important link between our spirit, our mind, our biology, and healing on all levels. One client developed testicular cancer at age twenty-two. He was a very angry guy. His doctor asked him what he was so angry about and he said that his parents had divorced, and he was unable to talk to either of them for two years. He just sat and boiled in his own anger until he manifested the cancer. It was his opinion that he had caused it himself. Another person who came to participate had a broken heart. I asked her what had happened, and she said her mother had died. I asked her when and she said seven years ago. She was stuck. She was really stuck. Her emotional body was also contributing to a very weakened immune system. I am not saying that a brain balancing is going to fix everybody's problems, but I will say, "It is a good start." It can facilitate moving us in the right direction to where constructive support can emerge.

The point of fact is that people need a dark or unconscious motivation to cause their own cancer. Living and moving in the light of balance we become more discerning and make better choices. Divorce is difficult, death isn't easy, but they always do seem to happen. We can stay strong if we stay balanced. And there is an old saying "A stitch in time saves nine."

I have had people say that on my table they get better insights about their own challenges and how to deal creatively with them.

Information is available or contained in all our energy. Energy is present in all living systems and things. If it has a pulse it has an electro-magnetic field. Your aura and field stretch three to six feet beyond your outstretched hands. That is your field, and it feels things. It picks things up. Clarity is functionality.

If you are holding a brick in your hand and a bird comes and lands on it, you may not even notice. Our signal-to-noise ratio is best set with the least disturbance to it. More noise, lower energy levels, fight or flight have a chronically deafening effect on our lives. A body-mind in balance can relax quicker, reflect better, plan better, and execute at a higher level of efficiency. Thoughts are things and often carry an emotional charge to the biology of the body. Be cool, be kind, be compassionate and keep your cells rotating in a clockwise direction. They are healthy. Be men, be nasty, be a bad ass and do these consistently and you will generate a bad condition.

Brain Body Balancing Used Together with Reiki

The true depth, power and promise of any healing system can only be realized by living it and by applying its principles to ourselves and then, of course, to others. Our natural inclinations towards wholeness have been stolen from a large percentage of us due to the onslaught of drug advertisements on television and radio, and the, sometimes underhanded, nature of the whole pharmaceutical industry and its suppression of natural modalities. Instant pain relief, instant and fast foods result in instant karma and the results for too many people. I have made sufficient reference to this in other sections of this manual.

It is important to mention that Dr. Usui, the founder of Reiki, was, most importantly, a dedicated Buddhist and accomplished martial arts teacher and healer. Healers are born and then many are trained. Weekend workshops are effective for some training of sorts, but often masters dedicate their whole lives to a system, 24/7. They live in the Tao, The Way, often at the expense of material wealth and stature.

Reiki Defined

Reiki is a spiritual or energetic healing process for balancing and harmonizing all aspects of a person, mind, body, spirit, and emotions. It is a gentle hands-on process that does not include pressure, manipulation, or massage. Universal life force energy, Source directed by life force energy and or just spiritual energy is used to define it.

REI:
Divinity, Wisdom and Knowledge of the Universe. A Higher Intelligence that understands cause and effect and how to heal.

KI:
The life force, which animates all living things.

Dr. Mikao Usui (1865-1926)

Dr. Usui, a Japanese Buddhist Priest, is the founder of the system. Originally Reiki was an oral tradition that first sprung out from his energy and ethics, so limited information is known about him. Stories have survived of his unique abilities, which truly grew out of his compassion, Buddhist principles, his meditation practice, and his studies of the martial arts. We might say that included many different martial arts systems. It should be noticed that Dr. Usui completed a three-year Zen Buddhist training that culminated in his achieving enlightenment (satori). He reached this state and empowered Reiki one hundred years ago on a very different planet earth. This difference will be defined later in this essay.

Having spent most of his life meditating, training and doing healing, Dr. Usui decided eventually that it was important to pass along his discoveries to other people. Dr. Hayashi was one of the recipients of his generosity and development. When Dr. Hayashi gave successful treatments to a Hawaiian woman visiting Japan, he succumbed to her request to train her. Her name was Hawayo Takata and she stayed and lived with Dr. Hayashsi's family to learn the system and way of life. She stayed long enough to be effective and, upon returning to Hawaii, opened the first Reiki clinic in America in 1938. She promoted an oral tradition and, although those traditions moved slowly, she eventually went on to train others who began to influence the spread of the work.

The number of systems that have been developed around the world that work with universal energy are simply far, far too many to mention. For example, there are over 200 chiropractic techniques within the chiropractic system. Quantum Healing, Polarity work, Lightwave, Ananda healing, Deeksha, are just a few of the systems developed that are not using massage or manipulation, but rather a form of energy transfer or channeling of energies. In my estimation, the greatest difference of the body, mind, and spirit systems of the East, is the true commitment to the individual's own development. The martial arts simply transcend any Western programs for exercise. Thousands of years of tradition go into its heart and soul, into its muscles and marrow. There is a difference between mastery and having a license, like the difference between a fine artist and someone coloring with a crayon.

A person whose physical body can learn the mysteries of ki or chi and who practices meditation is going to have potentially, a greater natural ability to transfer this energy. Early in my career as a bodyworker, one of my clients who lost the use of his legs as a result of a car accident visited a Tai Chi Master. He returned able to stand with support. This was quite amazing for me to observe.

Brain Body Balancing is, I believe now as I write this in October of 2017, a focused piece of technology that can absolutely be integrated into Reiki sessions and many, many systems of hands-on healing. Why? Because we live in an environment that produces too much stress which leaves all of us in a perpetual state of fight or flight. By doing the "Pulse" we are moving the brain very gently inside the cranium and facilitating a reset of brain body priorities. We can release the fight or flight mechanism and restore synchronization.

Hundreds of test cases of persons who are unable to get relief from traditional chiropractic joined a study and received the bio-energetic synchronization technique (B.E.S.T.). This is also a brain balancing process. Patients in this study had previously received a minimum of six months of chiropractic care without success. 85% of these patients responded to this new work approach. Alphabiotics also has produced many, many miracles.

The point is, if you are going to be interacting with the body, mind, and spirit of an individual, you can simply add this technique to communicate with the brain, gently and powerfully.

You can use Reiki and Brain Body Balancing to achieve a higher level, a deeper level of healing. The universal energies that are being beautifully introduced into a person's energy field will simply penetrate and facilitate better.

Inappropriate stress states of fight or flight drive a hard bargain. They insist and persist. If you measure the leg length of most teenagers there is a noticeable majority out of balance. The pace, complexity and toxicity of our lives and environment are truly overwhelming today. Americans ingest 80% of the world's painkillers. This is crazy and stupid, take your pick.

We must have more mindfulness; more people to brain body balance with one another. We need it now. At times I have spent as little as five minutes balancing chakras, grounding and pulsing only to receive an email hours later saying to me "My God, I feel better than I have in years." I imagine that this person has been locked into a stress state for years and now finally they have synchronization. Now imagine if on top of the brain body synchronization one could run those beautiful life force energies, how much more healing can be done?

Once you become familiar with Brain Body Balancing and the feeling of synchronization, you will want to have it in conjunction with any other bodywork. It is so easy, gentle, and powerful and takes just a few minutes to facilitate. Let's do Reiki and add Brain Body Balancing to your sessions.

The emphasis on Dr. Usui's teaching was as much about a spiritual awakening as on purely physical healing. This is a whole system for integration of body, mind, and spirit. The intent is to achieve a state of balance, which results in 100% integration of your body, mind, and spirit.

One hundred years ago the planet was in a more pristine state. We did not have power lines and complex electronic transmissions, microwaves, cell towers, cell phones, etc. People lived closer to the land and breathed better air. Bodies were not prone to going into fight or flight as we observe today.

For maintenance, a 10 to 12-minute Brain Body Balancing can be done once or twice a week. This produces a very powerful energetic adjustment and balancing for busy people. Full Reiki sessions with Brain Body Balancing can be enjoyed when time is permitting. Of course, having a full Reiki session and including a 12-minute Brain Body Balancing I believe, will meet the demands of the modern client. Also, Reiki practitioners can train their clients to do Brain Body Balancing in between visits. This will help spread the idea and activities of holistic principles.

If you have forgotten what it is to be in synchronization, we have a wonderful way to remind you and help you maintain this by receiving sessions and hopefully learning to facilitate them. We are presently hoping and imagining that Brain Body Balancing will become a more popular and integrated part of our culture's wellness practices.

CHAPTER 4

Essays

Morphogenetic Fields
The Hundredth Monkey

by Ken Keyes, Jr.

No copyright filed, free use is expressed

The Japanese monkey, Macaca fuscata, has been observed in the wild for a period of over 30 years. In 1952, on the island of Koshima, scientists were providing monkeys with sweet potatoes dropped in the sand. The monkeys liked the taste of the raw sweet potatoes, but they found the dirt unpleasant.

An 18-month-old female named Imo found she could solve the problem by washing the potatoes in a nearby stream. She taught this trick to her mother. Her playmates also learned this new way and they also taught their mothers.

Before the eyes of the scientist observers, this cultural innovation was gradually picked up by various monkeys; between 1952 and 1958 all the young monkeys learned to wash the sandy sweet potatoes to make them more palatable.

Only the adults who imitated their children learned this social improvement. Other adults kept eating the dirty sweet potatoes.

Then something startling took place. In the autumn of 1958, a certain number of Koshima monkeys were washing sweet potatoes - the exact number is not known. Let us suppose that when the sun rose one morning there were 99 monkeys on Koshima Island who had learned to wash their sweet potatoes.

Let's further suppose that later that morning, the hundredth monkey learned to wash potatoes.

THEN IT HAPPENED!

By that evening almost everyone in the tribe was washing sweet potatoes before eating them somehow due to the added energy of this hundredth monkey.

A most surprising thing observed by these scientists was that the habit of washing sweet potatoes then jumped over the sea - colonies of monkeys on other islands and the mainland troop of monkeys at Takasakiyama began washing their sweet potatoes.

Thus, when a certain critical number achieves awareness, this new awareness may be automatically communicated from mind to mind.

Although the exact number may vary, this Hundredth Monkey phenomenon means that when only a limited number of people know of a new way, it may remain the conscious property of these people.

But there is a point at which if only one more person tunes-in to a new awareness, the field is strengthened so that this awareness is picked up by almost everyone!

Let's Build the Field

There is mounting evidence that as more and more people learn or do something it becomes easier for others to learn or do it. In one experiment, British biologist Rupert Sheldrake took three short, similar Japanese rhymes – one a meaningless jumble of disconnected Japanese words, the second a newly composed verse and the third a traditional rhyme known by millions of Japanese. Neither Sheldrake nor the English schoolchildren he got to memorize these verses knew which was which, nor did they know any Japanese. The most easily learned rhyme turned out to be the one well known to Japanese. This and other experiments led Sheldrake to postulate that <u>there is a field of habitual patterns that links all people, which influences and is influenced by the habits of all people.</u> This field contains (among other things) the pattern of that Japanese rhyme. The more people have a habit pattern – whether of knowledge, perception, or behavior – the stronger it is in the field, and the more easily it replicates in a new person. In fact, it seems such fields exist for other entities too, like birds, plants, even crystals. Sheldrake named these phenomena *morphogenetic fields* – fields that influence the pattern or form of things. [Source: *"Morphic Fields and Morphic Resonance: An Introduction"* by Rupert Sheldrake, Feb 2005]

First, developing the manpower to get going with learning to do the brain balancing is our aim. Then, of course, as more concerned parents, partners, bodyworkers, Reiki practitioners, energy workers of all types and varieties see the wisdom of utilizing the "Pulse" and the Brain Body Balancing, the faster the wave will travel. As much as possible our intention of training as many people out of the pool of participants will surely cause amplification.

The following statement was uttered first in the late 70's: that we realize now that more scientists are open to living systems theory and more quantum evaluations.

Most biologists take it for granted that living organisms are nothing but complex machines governed by the known laws of physics and chemistry. I myself use to share this point of view. But, over the period of several years, I have come to see that such an assumption is difficult to justify. For when so little is actually understood, there is an open possibility that at least some of the phenomena of life depend on laws or factors as yet unrecognized by physical science.   [Source: Rupert Sheldrake, page 9, The Hypothesis of a New Science of Life]

The organistic or holistic philosophy provides a context for what could be yet a more radical revision of mechanistic theory.

It is interesting to note that Rupert Sheldrake wrote his book, *A New Science of Life*, during his stay at Shantivanan Ashram in southern India. He spent a few years there. The focus was a synthesis or blending of Vedanta, a Hindu philosophy, with the essence of Christian philosophy. It does appear that the concept of morphogenetic fields is still being defined. It is agreed that this field is responsible for the organization and form of material or physical systems. The question is "Does the M field have structure itself?" This is yet to be determined.

However, if thousands of rats were trained in a lab in London to perform a task and then the speed of learning was reduced later in a lab in New York, we are left to wonder how our small group of dedicated brain balancers can create a wave that will have raised consciousness to ripple out across the planet.

Biological morphogenesis is defined as the coming into being of characteristics and specific forms of living organisms.

Since biological systems can adapt, we want to see them adapt upward towards a higher order allowing each individual full access to the neocortex enabling them to function more as a whole.

In an ashram life, where people can spend an hour meditating twice a day, the need for stress management tools diminish. This meditation practice is difficult to sustain in our busy lives. However, stealing away for 12 minutes two or three times a week if possible, we believe can be life altering.

Energy-and the model for energy is by necessity an open system. The deepest levels of cause or source are yet to be discovered. We now know a bit about the space inside the atom, that it is 99.99% space. The universe is a vast space. Matter and the materialist view do not accept any theories of non-material causal agents. Man is a machine to them, and their medicine is pharmaceuticals.

Dr. Bruce Lipton has discovered that the nucleus is not the brain of the cell, but rather like a parts store within it. If you remove the nucleus from a cell it may go on living for days or weeks. However, if you damage the membrane, the cell may instantly die. The brain, he says, is in the environment or the self. Dr. Lipton stopped teaching cellular biology to medical students because he now believed that the medical belief structures, theories, principles, have been built upon sand. This is, in essence, a statement that all pharmaceutical medicine is based in fiction. They believe the nucleolus to be the brain. The pharmaceutical industry also has one of the deepest, darkest, strongest, and most powerful corporate mechanisms to enforce their control and domination.

I met Dr. Gordon who developed a little black box about the size of pack of cigarettes using scalar wave technology. Dr. Gordon, who was scheduled to have a heart transplant, became so healthy after using his device, that he called off the surgery and rode his bicycle across country to make a point. Some months later the FDA came and shut down production and distribution of his little healing device. It was bad for business. Which business? Big Pharma. It was also sad to hear about his death shortly thereafter. I am inclined to think he died of a broken heart. Best to get healthy and stay healthy. Amen

On Getting Zapped

Years ago, I encountered a woman in my practice who was suffering from chronic fatigue. She worked all day on a computer, came home, watched T.V. and then went to bed and slept underneath an electric blanket. This was a bad idea for her nervous system, for her electromagnetic energy. She was getting zapped and it was costing her, her own life. The electrical signals of her nervous system and subtle energies of the meridians and chakras were being bombarded constantly. In 1936 a scientist from Yale, used voltmeters to test the electromagnetic fields of the body. That was Dr. H.S. Burr. He said that electricity is the way that nature behaves. When electric current flows through a conductor or wire or a nerve path, a magnetic field is created. Usually this is termed an electromagnetic field.

Our electromagnetism is paramount to good health. We need to think of ourselves as an energy being. It is probably more accurate to say that you are a soul that has a person and not a person who has a soul. It may also be said that you are probably an electrical field that has a body and not a body that has a field.

This is reflected in modern diagnostic procedures of electrocardiograms for the heart, electroencephalograms for the brain, and magnetic resonance imaging (MRI's) for the body. Oriental systems call the energy chi. The yogis call this energy prana. Yin energy moves out to the extremities and yang energies move in toward the organs. The balance of yin and yang energy is our state of health or dis-ease. Although Western medicine is skeptic about acupuncture, in China they perform brain surgery using acupuncture instead of anesthesia. These acupuncture points are twenty-five times more conductive than other areas or points on the body. Although you can't see an acupuncture point you sure can feel them.

It is interesting to know that a solar flare can knock out communication systems and cause wires to burst into flames. A direct hit from a solar flare caused extensive damage in 1859.

The solar storm of 1859 (also known as the "Carrington Event") was a powerful geomagnetic storm during solar cycle 10 (1855-1867). A solar coronal mass ejection (CME) hit Earth's magnetosphere and induced one of the largest geomagnetic storms on record on September 1-2, 1859. The associated "white light flare" in the solar photosphere was observed and recorded by British astronomers Richard C. Carrington(1826-

1875) and Richard Hodgson (1804–1872). The storm caused strong auroral displays and wrought havoc with telegraph systems. The now-standard unique IAU identifier for this flare is SOL1859-09-01.

A solar storm of this magnitude occurring today would cause widespread electrical disruptions, blackouts, and damage due to extended outages of the electrical grid. The solar storm of 2012 was of similar magnitude, but it passed Earth's orbit without striking the planet, missing by nine days.

Presently We are Having Many Influences Due to the Sun

Many of us are experiencing symptoms such as fatigue, headaches, etc., from the magnetic influence of these fields. We know that more children are born on full moons and more people are arrested, but did you know that more cases of chest pain and arrhythmias occur around the full moon or intensified solar flares? Nowadays, it is considered by some to be potentially dangerous to work in an airplane because of the gamma rays produced by the sun and radiation from the plane. We are wired to respond to the electric universe, all of it, planets, moons, stars, suns, and for some the power pole outside your house. A friend once told me that when she went to the country to visit family and friends, when she left Seattle and the power poles outside her home, her back immediately stopped hurting. I know that the cell towers can really mess with radio reception. Animals respond to changes within the earth's surface before instruments can register. Medical visionaries predict that biophotonic energy emitted from our bodies will soon be used to diagnose us.

Our bodies are 75% water. Dr. Masaru Emoto, who has done amazing tests with water, found that the crystalline structure of water responds to words like love or kindness or gratitude. This would seem to indicate that the water in our bodies responds as well to our thoughts and others' thoughts, minds, and energy either positively or negatively.

Electro-pollution is a fact in our lives. The over-stimulation of the sympathetic nervous system is keeping us in fight or flight response. Cell phones can cause major problems in our lives by disrupting the glands in our face and head. Incidents of leukemia in children, is far greater when they live near power lines.

Many well-respected historians believe that the Romans killed themselves with lead. They used lead containers when making wine. The acidic grapes pulled the lead out into solution. They used heavy metal in almost everything including painting walls.

They died uninformed. So too we are doing this dying by degrees, now with invisible electronic toxins.

One of the things about electro-pollution is that it is silent, has no smell, is invisible and does not leave any mess to clean up except for our health. We are being affected thousands of times greater than our grandparents. Get away from the EMF's and often health symptoms disappear. Do not wait for the government to come in and protect you, they would rather put a smart meter on your house. These are dangerous, have high levels of radiation, and work as surveillance devices. Your doctor is happy to remove your thyroid or parathyroid glands so don't worry, they won't take away your cell phone.

On a cellular level, messages from cell to cell can get confused. Cells may send out signals to your system, but the confusion of electro-pollution causes mistranslation. Cells come unglued. Cells break down and this can run deep into our DNA. Cancer is more prevalent in children who live near stepped-down transformers (barrel type devices mounted outside some homes).

Dr. David Carpenter M.D., Dean of the School of Public Health at the state university of New York, believes 30% of childhood cancer is caused by EMP exposure. It does not take much. Existing safe exposure limits are ridiculously low and set by persons of the conspiracy. The accumulation of evidence is overwhelming. The list of possible health disorders is too long to mention here.

The book *Zapped,* by Anne Louise Gittleman, is a great book to read to become much better informed about how to adapt through greater awareness, self-defense, blocking, and by empowering ourselves through diet. I know I will share this great book with all my friends.

The bottom line is, if you are having any health challenges you need to talk to a naturopath or a wellness practitioner to help determine a treatment strategy to find a cause.

Children are not going to know, doctors are not going to ask, we must become better at self-awareness. Staying in balance in homeostasis can only improve our chances at wholeness and well-being. Being balanced allows the wisdom of the body to perform the wisdom of life.

Last week a gentleman came to see me because he was having low back and hip pain. The first thing I noticed when he got on the table was a circle in the right hip pocket of his jeans. He kept a can of chewing tobacco there. I pulled it out and told him to use the front pocket. I saw him in a store a few days later and he looked great. He smiled at me. Although it was not electrical, the can was detrimental and caused his sciatica. The same day, I released a gal from her electric blanket. Next time I saw her she was much better.

The Chakras

My search for chakras at the Stanwood WA library turned up 120 hits for books and CDs on the subject. Therefore, I will not be going on a very deep journey here because the research is available elsewhere. I am offering some basic ideas about each of the chakras and some antidotal stories about my personal observations of these all too invisible, intangible energy vortexes that people have been talking about for thousands of years.

The chakras, or the word for them in Sanskrit, means "wheels." They represent vortices of the dynamic whirling forces in the subtle body. Chakras, correspond to nerve centers in the body, are busy distributing Prana (energy) to both the physical and subtle bodies. Chakras are the organs of our subtle bodies. They step down energy from Spirit and move it to the body. They also pick up energies from the environment as well as reflect our state of wellness. Some systems of Eastern yoga and religions consider that when our chakras are fully developed, this is a step or progression toward a higher consciousness or unity.

It is an ancient way, and the imagery is considered accurate. The chakras depict an individual's maturation as he or she raises energies from the base, or lower chakras, to the higher chakras. It is optimal to have all your chakras aligned, cleared, and balanced. Master the chakras and you master your life.

1st Chakra/Red

The 1st chakra deals with energies and lessons of survival. This chakra represents the earth element. The color associated with this chakra is red. This chakra has been deeply imprinted and energized by family, community, and country by the time one reaches adult life. A healthy balanced base chakra will reflect a beautiful red color with some white in it. When a person has issues affecting this chakra, it will also become enlarged and have more of a murky red color. The base chakra, also called root chakra, is a foundation for our mental and emotional health. One might say as the Mayan people reflect their levels of consciousness, that our lower chakras reflect our relationship with the tribe. It is important to derive support from the tribe we come from. It is also important that they do not limit us.

I received a call from a friend in California to please do some healing for a mutual friend in Seattle. As I worked with her, I could not get a pulse on her first or root chakra. I suspected that her spirit was preparing to leave the body. The next week my friend called again and said that our friend was in the hospital, he asked me to go see her and mentioned that he had spoken to no less than seven psychics who all said she would pull through. I suggested that she was on her way out and a few hours later she made her transition. I think she was very happy to go; she had had a full life and was ready to return home.

Another story, a dear friend of mine contacted me to do some remote energy clearing because she was feeling extremely weak. Although I had cleared many cords from her root chakra, she wound up going to the hospital and receiving 2 pints of blood. I was very surprised that the cords were attached to her root chakra. After she got out of the hospital, she contacted me and informed me that her son-in-law had passed away. She had spent two weeks at the hospital at his bedside before he terminated. Of course, I cannot prove this, but I'm thinking that the son-in-law was not interested in making a transition, and, consequently, he was cording her root chakra. When she went into the hospital, they could not find a cause for the blood loss. It has now been seven years and, although I work with her at least every 3 to 6 months, she has never been corded at her root chakra again. All of this makes me a true believer in subtle energies and the power of the will to survive even if it is misdirected.

2nd Chakra/Orange

The 2nd chakra has creativity and sexuality as the key ideas or associated energies. It is also considered our relationship center. The color associated with this chakra is orange. This chakra does not activate until the individual is about seven years old.

I know two people, one man and one woman, who tested out-of-balance with no energy in their 2nd chakras. I have known them for at least 15 years (they do not know each other) and they have been very stagnant by my impression: with not much evolution and no love relationships. They lack creativity. The woman literally asked the universe to close down this chakra because of a bad divorce and a disinterest in being intimate again. It is my impression that this was a bad decision.

Walter Russell, renowned scientist, sculptor, artist, and musician, said that religious people like priests and nuns often become great scholars, but very rarely become great artists. Many of them suffer as well by imposing something very unnatural like celibacy in their lives. Nuns suffer from way above average levels of ovarian cancer. Could be you just can't fool Mother Nature.

3rd Chakra/Yellow

The 3rd chakra is often considered our power center: a center for our ego, personality, and self-esteem. This chakra usually blossoms at puberty, although nowadays we are generally seeing children that seem to be rewiring our ideas and understandings about being, creativity and personal power. I personally know a five-year-old who I believe has all three of the first centers well charged and fully expressed. This center or solar plexus chakra completes the trinity of the lower three chakras. The world functions primarily from this center. Unfortunately, it is my impression that it is a dog eat dog world, and that this center needs to stand under the supervision of the heart. Magnetic people have an abundance of energy here and they attract well. They attract a lot, but again, having and being are two different things altogether.

4th Chakra/Green

Love, forgiveness, compassion are the key qualities associated with the heart chakra, the central chakra of the system. Everyone has one and much needs to be learned about it. I learned from one of my teachers, a great healer, that "the best way to protect your heart is to open it." An open heart will outperform an open mind. You don't have to be spiritual to be psychic and if you do open and advance spiritually through inner work, healing and development, your psychic abilities will open quite naturally and be guided by the wisdom of the heart.

Everyone will be challenged and perhaps will need to make daily choices based on fear or love, to react or to respond to persons, places, or things.

Once I stayed with a company too long. It went into bankruptcy and I was not compensated for the last six months of work there. I was very upset and realized after two and a half months, holding my thoughts about it and the personalities involved, meant I was holding a negative energy in my heart. This was having a very bad, total effect on my heart chakra, affecting my entire being.

I decided to try something different. I began working with a prayer called a Sanskrit Sloka. I decided every time I thought about the CEO or president of the company, that I would recite the Sloka. The prayer reads: "May all Beings be free of suffering, have equanimity and peace. The sloka, *Lokha somasta shukino bhavantu*, has been tremendously helpful for me for my personal energies and sense of completion of an exercise that I was involved with for five years. Most life issues like death, divorce, abuse, abandonment have heart centered resonance. Keep open, keep healing, and keep moving forward. *Lokha somasta shukino bhavantu*.

5th Chakra/Blue

Lessons related to will and self-expression.

Sound is associated with the 5th chakra. This is oriented toward self-expression and creative identity. This is our truth center. Generally speaking, although there are always exceptions to the rule, people who speak the truth have healthy 5th chakras. People who whine and complain a lot, will suffer tonally as a result. These imbalances are often expressed as throat and thyroid imbalances.

6th Chakra/Indigo

The 6th chakra is associated with light and the functions of this chakra often involve mature self-inquiry and self-reflection. It is obvious that the world is not famously over activated in this center, often referred to as the third eye. A healthy 6th chakra helps us see the big picture, gives us a sense of clarity and inner vision. The things that keep us from seeing clearly are limited beliefs and the collective and personal illusions that we all live with.

Key words for this chakra are the mind, insight, intuition, and wisdom. A balanced 6th chakra is a place where the emotions and intellect can be empowered.

Inner vision is not like watching television. It is the fluid movement of your life around, under or over the challenges of life. We can have a vision of moving forward under any circumstances. Sometimes moving forward can mean to quit or stop and then be fluid and flexible enough to change directions. Multidimensional and multi-talented people must be clear as to where to put their energy and for how long.

I stopped playing guitar completely for 14 years and then started again. I then wrote, composed, and recorded no less than six cd's, then organized twelve 50-minute guided meditation CD's. I then stopped playing guitar again and have not played for a few years. However, my creative processes continued, and I have since completed another book called *Be Clear Now, A Beginner's Guide to Pendulum Clearing*. Now I am working on organizing, writing, and teaching Alpha Brain Body Balancing and the Pulse, a key to whole brain function. My hope is to touch a million people through the people I train and those that they train and facilitate. Hidden talents emerge when we have stabilized our energies from the base chakras through the heart and into the mind. You will need more hours in a day to do all the things you want to do when you have raised your base energies from your lower centers up to the higher centers. And, by the way, we have not yet touched on the crown chakra where our contact with our I Am Presence and superconscious mind happens.

7th Chakra/Gold/White

Unity, Enlightenment, Spirituality, Clearing Ideas

This is known as the crown chakra. We set an intention to clear and balance our chakras, we strengthen our inner energy to optimize our health and well-being.

In that light, charge up when you can and always have a balance buddy to work with, them on you and vice versa. By honoring the request to "teach and train," find at least one other person to exchange with. You will always have a resource for this. When I did Alphabiotic training in Dallas, many came from around the country to get balanced. When they returned home there was often no one to work on them. Now we have a way and a wave to perpetuate the balance. Now we have a very gentle but powerful pulse to share. Thanks for helping!

Discovery of Chakra Clearing

Let me explain my discovery of how to use the circle and sign of the cross to clear negative energy.

When a client came for a session with me, I sensed a disturbance in her field, in her third eye chakra. I asked her if I could muscle test her and she agreed. I did a scan and when I placed by hand over the chakra, she went immediately weak. I asked her to close her eyes and made a circle and the sign of the cross over the chakra, with the intent to clear, align and balance this chakra. I asked her to take a deep breath and relax for a minute. When I muscle tested her again, she was all-clear.

It was then that she told me that she had had nightmares the night before that she thinks were related to watching a miniseries on television about the Book of

Revelations. The darkness of the program affected her negatively. My clearing here affected her positively. I might say that the "lights were turned back on."

When we balance the chakras, we draw a circle clockwise for the front of the chakra; when we draw the circle counterclockwise, we are affecting the back of the chakras. Then we draw a vertical line followed by a horizontal line. Visualizing the color sends another intent to restore, revitalize, and balance the chakras.

The longer we participate in any kind of healing, service, or practice and the more open we stay, we are intuitively guided. It was good for this client to have her faith restored by my noticing the disturbance and clearing it. She confirmed the insight by then reporting on the nightmares, which have since stopped. As we function in balance, in synchronization and alignment, we become more sensitive to energies, both positive and negative. Thus, we can become more helpful.

Word Energy Vibration

Every Time You Curse You Curse Yourself

We live in a vibrational universe. Thoughts are things on the mental plane and all-of-our-thoughts are creative. Thoughts are the building blocks of our universe. The personal creative process flows from thought to word to action. It is proven fact that people who pray live longer and have less depression. There is power in positive thinking. If you muscle-test someone saying the phrase "I love you," they will test very strong. The words "I'm sorry" make a person test weak. Can you imagine what the continued use of the F-bomb has on one's astral body? I never heard my parents curse. It is strange for me to hear just how common it is for people, especially women, to curse. Edgar Cayce said that 'It's not the things that you can see that are our problem; it is what you can't see. You cannot see it because it is on the astral plane. Karma, crap, and cooties are all hanging around just waiting for an opportunity to be born. They would infiltrate our reality until we create a strong enough defense to release them into the light of reason, into the light of awareness, into the light of forgiveness, into the light of love. Everyone has a shadow. It comes with the territory.

A client of mine left her husband because he was a drunk, abusive, and was a real control freak. He promised her he would haunt her and never let her have another relationship. She hooked up with another man right away and was attacked by his (the new guy's) ex-wife/girlfriend who tried to take her head off. She was in serious pain a week after the event. Yet she could not wait to get re-involved. I really wanted her to wait and have a period of readjustment, but it was not my business to tell her. I believe she could have made a better choice if she first established a more powerful connection with her own "I AM Presence." We can ask assistance of our guardian angels to help bring the right people, places, and things to our experience. If we don't ask our higher light then rest assured your other angels will do it for you; yes, the dark ones. Do not get me wrong. You can learn a lot in the negative. It is probably going to affect us anyway, but why invite it? At the time Saddam Hussein invaded Kuwait, I was helping to produce a television show, an infomercial, which immediately went down the tubes. Four and a half years and a minimum of half a million dollars went down with it. I had never even heard of this Hussein guy. Planet Earth is a difficult school. Or let's say it this way, if you don't stay on top of your game here, chances are you are going to come up empty sometimes.

My teacher once told us we must invoke the light immediately upon arising. We do not have to do it at that exact time of awakening; we actually have 30 seconds to get it done. Why? Because when we sleep, we travel through the astral plane. That is the place where ghosts and goblins like to hang out. It's a bad neighborhood. In the teaching of the ascended masters they make a clear point of emphasizing just why we need to invoke the light daily. Light, our lives depend on it. I would imagine that if people would make this one small and meaningful change and eliminate the bad sounds, the curse words, that new patterns of light and beauty would emerge. One time, I was sitting by myself playing my guitar and singing a song called the "Bud and the Rose;" afterwards I went into the house. A friend came over and welcomed me, giving me a hug and said," you smell like a rose." Could it be that simple? Probably is!

The point being, if singing is focusing an image and an energy vibration that manifests an essence like a smell or fragrance, then the opposite must be true. Don't take my word for it. Make a commitment to having a purely positive energy vibration that blesses instead of the opposite. Take the challenge with yourself.

Rise up like the phoenix out of its own ashes. Raise your vibration through conscious sound/word energy vibration. And good vibes to you too!

The Seven Levels
of Personal Consciousness

By Richard Barrett

[The following pages on the Seven Levels of Personal Consciousness have been generously loaned to our project by Richard Barrett]

Every human being on the planet evolves and grows in consciousness in seven well-defined stages. Each stage focuses on a particular existential need that is common to the human condition. These seven existential needs are the principal motivating forces in all human affairs. The level of growth and development of an individual depends on the ability to satisfy his or her needs.

The seven stages in the development and growth of personal consciousness are summarized in the following table and described in detail in the subsequent paragraphs. The *Seven Levels of Personal Consciousness* table should be read starting from the bottom and working up.

The first three levels of consciousness focus on our personal self-interest satisfying our physiological needs for security and safety, our emotional needs for love and belonging, and our need to feel good about ourselves through the development of a sense of pride in who we are, and a positive sense of self-esteem. Abraham Maslow referred to these as "deficiency" needs. We feel no sense of lasting satisfaction from being able to meet these needs, but we feel a sense of anxiety if these needs are not met. When these needs are paramount in our lives, we are conditioned by the expectations of those around us—by our social environment (the family and the culture we were brought up in). We align and are loyal to the groups with which we identify.

The focuses of the fourth level of consciousness is on transformation—learning how to manage, master or release the subconscious, fear-based beliefs that keep us anchored in the lower levels of consciousness. During this stage of our development, we establish a sense of our own personal authority, and our own voice. We are able to let go of our need to identify with our social environment because we have learned how to master our deficiency needs. We now choose to live by the values and beliefs that resonate deeply with who we are. We begin the process of self-actualization by focusing on our individuation.

Level	Focus	Motivation	
7	Service	Devoting your life to self-less service in pursuit of your passion or purpose and your vision.	
6	Making a Difference	Actualizing your sense of purpose by cooperating with others for mutual benefit and fulfillment.	
5	Internal Cohesion	Finding meaning in your life by aligning with your passion or purpose and creating a vision for your future.	
4	Transformation	Becoming more of who you really are by uncovering your authentic self and aligning your ego with your soul.	
3	Self-esteem	Feeling a sense of personal self-worth	Underlying anxieties about not being respected and not being enough
2	Relationship	Feeling a sense of love and belonging	Underlying anxieties about not being accepted and not being loved
1	Survival	Feeling secure and safe in the world	Underlying anxieties about not being safe or secure and not having enough
		HEALTHY MOTIVATIONS	**UNHEALTHY MOTIVATIONS**

THE SEVEN LEVELS OF PERSONAL CONSCIOUSNESS

The upper three levels of consciousness focus on our need to find meaning and purpose in our existence: actualizing that meaning by making a difference in the world and leading a life of selfless service. Abraham Maslow referred to these as "growth" needs. When these needs are fulfilled, they do not go away. They engender deeper levels of motivation and commitment. During this stage of our development, we increasingly develop the capacity to stand back and reflect on the strengths and limitations of our own ideology. We learn how to become our own self-witness and develop an inner compass that intuitively guides us into making life-affirming decisions.

Individuals that focus *exclusively* on the satisfaction of the lower needs, tend to live self-centered, shallow lives. They are significantly influenced by the anxieties and fears they hold about satisfying their deficiency needs.

Individuals that focus *exclusively* on the satisfaction of the higher needs tend to lack the skills necessary to remain grounded and operate effectively in the physical world. They can be ineffectual and impractical when it comes to taking care of their basic needs.

The most successful individuals are those who balanced both their "deficiency" needs and their "growth" needs. They operate from Full Spectrum Consciousness. They are trusting of others, are able to manage complexity, and can respond or rapidly adapt to all situations.

Full Spectrum Consciousness

Full Spectrum individuals display all the positive attributes of the Seven Levels of Personal Consciousness:

- They master survival consciousness by developing the practical skills required to ensure their physical security and safety.

- They master relationship consciousness by developing the interpersonal relationship skills required to engender a sense of belonging and being loved.

- They master self-esteem consciousness by developing a positive sense of self-worth and a personal sense of pride in who they are and how they perform.

- They master transformation consciousness by learning how to manage, master or release the subconscious and conscious, fear-based beliefs that keep them anxious about satisfying their deficiency needs.

PART TWO

MIND

CHAPTER 5

Introduction to the Mind

What did the Buddha say "I think therefore I AM?" Is it the great illuminator or that which slays a man, mind? One must engage with the practice of mindfulness in any one of its multitudes of forms or be forever compromised by culture, habits, patterns, and ancestral memory. In this section we are simply offering a few possibilities and referencing modern as well as ancient models. These essays form the nucleus of the work that I have participated in some measure in my life. Healing came from here to me. The subject of "mind" is a bottomless ocean and here we are simply observing a few grains of sand that have been left to dry in the summer sun and upon a beach of chance.

It is the hope of the writer to introduce areas of study for further research and empowerment. I encountered an older couple who, after living on Maui for 30 years, had never heard of Huna. So sad! What the kahunas were capable of will both surprise and delight you in the essay on the "Introduction of the Huna." The hermetic saying of "The lips of wisdom are sealed except to the ears of understanding" will facilitate a deepening and appreciation of a wonderful culture that we could derive a greater meaning—if we would but open our ears today.

It is always a good time to observe the influence that the mind, the beliefs, the programs that direct us from the subconscious, have upon our experience. It is key to enter into the map room and make a few subtle changes along the way to influence greater possibilities. Welcome, dive in at your own pace and, if a light goes off somewhere, kick your shoes off and enjoy the view. We are not writing anything in stone here but, more or less, just whispering in the wind to open, examine and be empowered by the knowledge that we are all the captains of our own ships. Our destiny is in our own hands and minds.

CHAPTER 6

Essays

Seven Principles of Hermetic Philosophy

"If you want to know the secrets of the universe. think of energy, frequency and vibration" - Nicola Tesla

"The lips of wisdom are sealed except to the ears of understanding."
The Kybalion

"Minds are like parachutes; they only work when they are open."
Anonymous

The pyramids on the Giza plateau sing of days gone by and a wonder of how they came to be, and why. Some say that at the fall of Atlantis many escaped to Egypt and other places on the planet. What is also speculated or confirmed depending on your choice of sources, that from here came our ancient sciences of astronomy, astrology, mathematics (Pythagoras went there for initiation), the knowledge of herbs, medicine and much more. In the ancient days, there were healers, shamans, medicine men and women who were generally priests or monks, with deep convictions to the integrity of their arts. Today we have the pharmaceutical industry which runs the program. I will let your mind fill in the rest.

The Seven Hermetic Principles have been left intact since that ancient time. Even today our modern science and the quantum concepts are affirming their substance and reality. These are the Seven Principles outlined in the Kybalion whose origin is mysterious, ancient, and profound.

1. The Principle of Mentalism

The One, the All is Mind. The Universe is a mental space.

Do you really want hemispheres to be locked in an inappropriate stress state?

Practice mindfulness instead when you are in harmony and balance.

2. Principle of Correspondence

As above, so below, as below so above

"That which is below is like that which is above & that which is above is like that which is below to do the miracles of one thing." Hermes Trismegistus, Emerald Tablet

"As above, so below" and apply it to the existence of consciousness and creativity, then indeed we could follow it all the way up and see that humans are a mirror of Godhead, the singular consciousness and creative potential.

The macrocosm and the microcosm are referred, revered above. The planes of existence above, of spirit and higher dimensions have a correspondence on us below. How this relates to the neocortex of the brain will unfold more in the next principle.

I want to share with you a vision of current world transformation that is now in its infancy, but it is going to grow considerably in the coming years. We are being given an opportunity to awaken as never before. Why? Because the time is right. The three most supportive planets in our solar system just synchronized with each other and struck a gong that sent a tone ringing through the whole universe. Jupiter Neptune and Chiron are the most supportive planets for our efforts to get inside of things, for seeing and feeling things, and for taking the next step in evolution as a natural gesture that will open the way to the future. Why is this critical? Because, for centuries we have lived a split existence. "The human has become split from a world above and below; we are like superheroes with amnesia, who got lost in their secret identities and forgot their powers." [Source: Cosmic Weather Report, Mark Borax and Elias Longsdale]

Everything in the cosmos is made of the substance of the cosmos.

3. The Principle of Vibration

Everything vibrates; everything is in motion, nothing rests. From molecules and atoms, electrons and worlds and universes, everything is in a vibratory motion. Westinghouse has proven that glass changes in density, a window will be thicker at the bottom than on the top if it sits around for a hundred years. In essence, they are saying that glass is a slow-moving liquid.

Being brain locked in a stress pattern that perturbs your healing signals to the body is a compromise to you vibrationally. You need to vibrate openly, properly and fully to be a whole person. The Pulse assists you to return to your normal and natural vibratory patterns. Let this vibration of balance orchestrate the wisdom of the body.

Among the most important skills in the work of the Druid mysteries is vibration, which is a particular mode or speaking or chanting names, words, and phrases of power. [Source: Michael Green, The Celtic Golden Dawn, page 34]

I personally use mantras before, during and after sessions. Some ancient mantras are easy to learn and provide great healing energy. These mantras can be sourced on the Internet:

Mrtujaya Mantra
Lokah Samastah
Gayatri Mantra

4. The Principle of Polarity

Everything is dual in nature. Everything has poles. Everything has its pairs of opposites.

In the human nervous system, we have sympathetic and parasympathetic branches. Skydiving and racecar driving are very sympathetic in nature and function; these activities are "fight or flight." Meditation and getting a massage are parasympathetic in nature; thought of as "rest and digest." People who can shift back and forth freely enjoy a greater degree of flexibility and health. An example of opposites is when two people stop at a red light: one person relaxes while the other chooses to release his foot off the brake, drive a couple of feet, then reapply the brake a number of times, expecting that this will accelerate the light to change. It just never works.

5. The Principle of Rhythm

Everything flows in and out. Everything has its tides. All things rise and fall. This is present in the affairs of the universe, suns, worlds, men, animals, mind, energy, and matter.

When you function using your whole brain, your sense of rhythm is undisturbed. You become balanced and free flowing. Being one with yourself allows to you engage in your environment with a greater sense of harmony. There is a greater chance for you to become one with nature when you are one with your Self.

6. The Principle of Cause and Effect

Every cause has an effect. Every effect has a cause. Everything happens according to law.

If you are locked in an inappropriate stress state, with power moving to one side of your body and weakness to the other side, the messages sent to the organs and glands will reflect this chaos. It has been observed in the study of cadavers that in most cases where there are diseased organs, there is a corresponding entrapment of the nerve flow to the organ. This results ultimately in dysfunction and disease. The endocrine system will suffer by a reduction of the appropriate hormones. When you are functioning optimally your body will produce a regenerative hormone known as DHEA. When you go into fight or flight mode, the adrenals produce a stress hormone called cortisol which, when it enters your bloodstream, affects blood sugar levels.

If you have come into contact with a saber-toothed tiger, you have a legitimate reason for being in a state of emergency—having to run for your life—and there is no problem with this physiological disposition. However, if all you are doing is sitting at a red light you will be healthier if you can just take a breath and relax for just a moment. Eventually the light will change. In other words, there is no sense spinning your wheels with the brakes on.

This is why it is ideal for families to learn how to contribute to one another by releasing the very harmful fight or flight mechanism.

7. The Principle of Gender

The Principle of Gender works in the direction of generation, regeneration, and creation. Everything and every person have both determinants. Every male has female properties, and every female has male properties.

There is nothing in the human kingdom that is more attractive, more beautiful, and more powerful than a being who lives a balance of these two life force energies.

We are living in an age of specialization. More and more, we are turning out educated people to work in systems that lack any sense of order and beauty.

Alcoholism, drug addition, prescription painkillers, and antidepressants are not the wave of the future. They are a wave of destruction for individuals, families, and communities.

Every time you balance someone you help reset the world.

Be bold, be brave, be innovative, and be balanced.

Cords

A cord is defined as "an energetic attachment that generally flows out of the solar plexus or first or second chakras on to the energy field of another person." Energetic cords can be very disabling to the individuals to whom they are attached. This is presently ALMOST completely overlooked by practitioners, doctors, and healers today. Recently, a friend told me she listened to a clairvoyant who is a practicing hypnotherapist who said that his practice is centered on cord removal.

There are some great resources for books on healing, chakras and alternative thought. Here are two examples for cord clearing that I use:

1. Call upon Archangel Michael whose primary job is to clear away all dark energies.
2. Visualize yourself holding scissors, a knife or sword and see or feel yourself cutting all the cords.

You might say that the first method of calling in Archangel Michael is an invocation; the second method is the intention visualized. When we do energy work and healing, we are all always acting as channels of some sort. Allow your higher self and guide committee to come through. They will come through and they will recycle those energies for us if your mind is clear and your intention is set.

I personally trust and believe in Archangel Michael, but I will not pretend to be sufficiently advanced to understand him and his function in the universe. Soon I hope to be otherwise and I will become angel-wise. All the work that we do through prayer, invocation and any and all methods of working upon our chakras, gives us the evolving abilities to stay clear and to help people clear themselves. It is a mysterious subject. I personally have to do clearing for other people because even though individuals live pure lives; they are still susceptible to these draining energies. Healthcare providers are the most susceptible and vulnerable to energetic cording.

The following is a contribution from Carole Conlon, master dowser and developer of the LifeWeaving system. http://Aynilifeweaving.com

> **Cords** are energy conduits or lines sent by someone else (close by, distant, over the phone, or even from a past life) that attach to a person and severely drain his or her energy. The person doing the cording can either be very needy and may not be

conscious of his or her act or may be doing it on purpose. The person being corded will experience an intense, sudden drop in energy—feeling fine one minute and possibly barely able to keep his or her eyes open the next.

When cords move through the *Clearing Macro*, the following occurs: a spiritual medical team removes the cords and heals the area; next the cord is ignited like a fuse with a flame of forgiveness and unconditional love, and then it burns back to the sender.

In conclusion, the process of learning to live cord free as well as becoming proficient at removing cords takes time to learn. I would assess that cords are somewhat astral in nature—beyond our physical body, etheric body, and causal body. Through brain body balancing, mindfulness, and practicing all types of methods of self-awareness we become more in tune. If you do not have a healing arts partner to work with, please contact me for support. This can be part of your education and illumination. It takes me just a few minutes to clear cords. I have some wonderful, well-directed and disciplined friends who still have challenges with cords from time to time. Very early in my career when I was in training in Hoshino Therapy at The Arthritis Foundation, I was told to learn to meditate. We often worked on people who were very imbalanced with layers and years of bad energy. Our meditation time daily was important to help neutralize the questionable cords and accumulation of unwanted energy.

A great resource to maintain a balance is to work with the 12 minute *I AM Meditation* on my web site. It is *free* at http://LifeSeedCodes.com.

On Brains and Minds

The Pulse and Brain Body Balancing is a communication of care, kindness and love.

We know very little about the nature of our minds. They are the basis of all experience, all our mental and social life, but we do not know what they are. Nor do we know their extent. The traditional view found all over the world is that the conscious life is part of a far larger animate reality. The soul is not confined to the head but extends throughout and around the body. It is linked to the ancestors, connected with the life of animals, plants, the earth and the heavens. It can travel out of the body in dreams and in trance. And at death, it can communicate with a vast realm of spirits of ancestors, animals, nature spirits, beings such as elves, fairies, elementals, demons, gods and goddesses, angels, and saints. [Rupert Sheldrake, The Hypothesis of the New Science of Life, Park Street Press]

That is a lot of communication. By contrast, for more than 300 years the dominant theory in the West has been that minds are located inside the head.

The information age is certainly wonderful, but as we can attest, it is drowning in big data, little data, and everything in between. As new items, texts, bills, apps, art and advice flow into our lives we are expected to make more and more and faster decisions than we have ever had to before. [Source: Daniel J. Levitin, *The Organized Mind*]

Seven Levels of Brain Function

7 Lowest-pre-reptilian
6 Reptilian
5 Pre-amphibian
4 Amphibian
3 Pre-mammalian
2 Mammalian
1 Neocortex of the brain.

Of the neocortex it is said that this is "your truly human brain."

According to David Hawkins, MD, PHD, page 83 of his book, the *Eye of I* essays, over 1/3 of the population has a brain that does not produce enough of the neurotransmitter serotonin to keep the individual from being depressed, from overeating, addicted or being out of behavioral control.

Rationality is further undermined by the biological fact that the old reptile and animal brain is still anatomically and functionally present, and its atavistic activity continues to exert a pervasive animal instinct that strengthens predatory tendencies and aggression.

The emotions of the animal are ever present and close to the surface. Or I should say, they bubble over from the lower levels of the brain and out into our reality as anger, aggression, control, manipulation, and fear. If we add in the programming and influences from video games, computer games and violent television, especially for the minds of developing children, we may be sowing seeds for disaster.

I am a proud father of two wonderful daughters. They have meaningful careers and now, in their early forties, they compete in bodybuilding and martial arts. Their mother and I divorced when they were 3 years and 1 ½ years old. Whenever they stayed with me on Friday, Saturday, and Sundays, they both received mini treatments every night at bedtime. I absolutely believe that the sessions really helped them developmentally. My daughter Alice graduated valedictorian of her high school and received a full academic scholarship to the University of North Carolina. My other daughter, Lynnea Faith, is always working for peace and liberation for friends and family. She will hop on a plane, rent a car, stay in a hotel then drive a few hours to catch a ferry to see a friend who is transitioning from this life. I have seen her do it a number of times, for a number of people. This is a rare example of a person whose brain and mind work near the heart.

Ida Rolf, the founder of Rolfing, a form of structural integration, said, "People are not a collection of stuff that abides, they are patterns that perpetuate themselves." John Lennon said, "All we are saying is give peace a chance." I am presently watching over two growing children age 7 and 10. They do go out of balance often and we do not let them stay there. Our promise to them presently is a promise of balance for a brighter future.

Brains are like snowflakes and there are no two identical in the universe. A recent study at the University of Chicago was done where each brain was carefully preserved and examined for microscopic evidence of age-related brain diseases. Each donor was vigorously tested and studied with batteries of tests for psychological and cognitive appraisals to medical, physical, and genetic tests. Hundreds of nuns participated in the study. When the study began, researchers expected to find a clear-cut link between cognitive decline and disease of the brain. They were completely wrong. Keeping a busy lifestyle into old age benefits the brain. Researchers were caught off guard by the results. There were many people with diseased tissue that were symptom free. Keeping busy and challenging the brain/mind was key to healthy function.

Also, there is a strong consensus that our brains are evolving and have come a long way in a few hundred years. Language is helpful for activation. I believe the introduction and use of brain entrainment systems are going to prove extremely helpful in this area. I personally use and recommend them to all my clients, friends, and family. Resources for this can be found at, www.project-meditation.org, www.centerpointe.com, and www.SacredAcoustics.com.

On the dark side or the flip side, negative psychological factors like loneliness, anxiety, depression have all contributed to a more rapid cognitive decline. Participants with diseased neural tissue, but no cognitive symptoms, had built up a reserve. Some areas of their brains had degenerated, while other areas had been well exercised; these compensated for the problem areas or had taken over those functions.

The more you keep the brain fit by challenging it and staying socially active, the more neural networks build new roadways to get around on.

Question: What does your brain need to stay healthy? Beyond nutrition, oxygen, and water, we need something equally important: we need one another. Normal brain function depends on the social web around us. Our neurons require other people's neurons. All your experiences in your life shape the details of your life. Who you are or what you wind up being or doing depends on where you have been and what has happened to you. You are a biological shapeshifter constantly rewriting your own paths and pathways, your own circuits. As much as you resonate with your tribe, family, profession, environment, astrology sign, your identity is fluid and moving because your neural patterns are changing so often throughout your whole life. You are a shapeshifter.

Your entire life of ups and downs, ins and outs, takes place inside the temple of your skull in the brain. My mother, who turned 94 on July 19th, 2017, has been in hospice now for three years. She is the most positive person I know at all of 70 pounds. She has a deep well of spiritual energy. We are not as hard-wired as we think and because our identity is so fluid and moving, this begs for the sanity, and the strategy, of staying brain balanced.

The following is a copy of an email I received from a company that offers brain entrainment technology, amazing stuff that I highly recommend. There are a few great companies out there like Equisync, HoloSync, and Sacred Acoustics.

> *"The human brain has 100 billion neurons, with each neuron connected to 10 thousand other neurons. Sitting on your shoulders is the most complicated object in the known universe."*
>
> Michio Kaku

Meditation and "Whole Brain Synchronization"

Deep Meditation offers your nervous system a super fertile atmosphere, triggering enormously positive transformations in your body and brain.

Just as higher levels of exercise force your body to strengthen and develop, the higher levels of deep neuro-stimulation and brain entrainment provided through meditation forces your nervous system into optimal performance.

Unlock Your Brain's Limitless Potential – The Benefits of Hemispheric Synchronization are Profound

Your entire nervous system and brain are transformed and reorganized on a higher level. A foundation of new neural pathways is constructed.

Your left and right brain hemispheres communicate to a degree never seen before, producing what doctors call whole brain functioning.

And, of course, there are all the wonderful benefits that we discussed earlier. Science really has only just discovered the tip of the iceberg in relation to this powerful, life-changing mind-tool.

Your brain has two hemispheres, left and right:

Left Hemisphere Thinking: Generally, more sequential, linear, logical, practical, mathematical, analytical, scientific, and time oriented.

Right Hemisphere Thinking: More non-linear, intuitive, abstract, big-picture focused, creative, and space oriented.

Most people use one hemisphere more than the other, creating an imbalance.

Numerous electroencephalograph (EEG) studies have shown that humanity's greatest philosophers, inventors, and artists use both brain hemispheres together, in unison.

Meditation works to balance both hemispheres of the brain, forcing them to work in harmony. Scientists call this "whole brain synchronization" and when achieved, your brain experiences extremely beneficial changes in hemispheric blood flow and **chemistry**.

During meditation, the grand central station-like cable of nerves connecting your two brain hemispheres, the **corpus callosum**, becomes deeply stimulated, much like a jogger's legs on a long run.

Due to the recently discovered, incredibly significant "**neuroplastic**" nature of the brain, meditation's **brain entrainment** enables this bridge-like structure, in addition to other inner **brain circuitry** like the feel-good **prefrontal-cortex**, to strengthen and grow.

What does this mean for you? Your **mind** will become more awakened, **focused**, deep, more **powerful** yet **peaceful**. By integrating both hemispheres of your brain and allowing them to work in sync, you will experience an increase in overall mental health, enhancing cognitive performance, **better memory** and **intellectual** functioning.

You will begin to notice a limitless supply of insightful **thoughts**, with far less **anger, anxiety, depression, addiction**. You will be happier, more optimistic, while feeling more "at one" with the world. All of these **benefits** build one on top of the other, accumulating over time.

Tap into a Deeper Level of Insight, Intelligence and Creativity

Meditation just might be the key to unlocking your untapped, limitless potential. Perhaps you were supposed to become the next Beethoven, Einstein, or Da Vinci?

While it is possible you may not end up a genius, you just might! The only way you will know for sure is if you give meditation a try. Although we have no idea what level of higher brain function you'll reach, we do know that those people who use this **technology** routinely tap into a whole range of extraordinary **abilities** they **never knew they had**.

About Sound

Some people equate Plato with the saying "In the beginning was the word, and the word was with God, and the word was God." Then of course, the Supreme Being said "Let there be Light," and you know what, "then there was Light," and from what I understand there was an abundance of it. Sound was the first thing emerging from the slumber of non-being. When the time for being, for creation, became present it was ushered in by sound. That is powerful! Everything in the physical universe has *vibration* and can be identified by its sound wave signature. In fact, our voiceprint is more identifiable than a fingerprint.

Source creates all things by sound. It is possible that on the mental plane that all thought produces sound. We are not empowered yet to be able to measure and record the sounds within a person's mind, but I AM sure a day will come when we will be able to do this. I had a friend that would read my mind, I Am serious about this, and often I was totally amazed at what she pulled out of it. I hope when we all reach this point that our minds are more beatific, poetic, and sublime. We must be "service to other" orientated. If the Divine Being said, "Let there be Light and there was Light" we can imagine that sound is the primary mechanism of Creation, the thing that is really turning the wheel is sound and of course, Light.

Mantras, powerful tools for transformation, have been utilized for thousands of years. I heard a story about a shaman who did a healing mantra for a friend for 120 days. He thought a healing would happen and the friend would stay, instead she passed on the evening of day 120. At first, disappointed, he received a dream where the friend told him how she was able to cross over in joy and anticipation and was reincarnating in a beautiful place, circumstance, with a wonderful family. She thanked him for introducing her to that mantra which she also chanted for 120 days.

When we vibrate these mantras through singing or listening, we affect a shift or increase of vibration or frequency. We chant the mantras not only for ourselves, but also for the whole planet. We achieve a balanced state, we extend our balance, the mantra radiates from us to bless and balance those whom we direct it towards. In this way we bring more light and love to the planet.

When we raise our frequency, we can heal more quickly. These healing vibrations unite the energetic, spiritual, and cellular bodies. By sounding our voices, we become peaceful, the wisdom of the physical body knows how to heal itself. To radiate more light and positive energy is the goal of the spiritual path. We activate and illuminate the body as we chant. We can move through the emotions of fear, shame, guilt, and anger to release the memory, density, and history to carry higher frequencies of pure energy and light.

Moola Mantra

Om Sat Chit Ananda Parabrahma Purushothama Paramatma Sri Bhagavati Sametha Sri Bhagavate Namaha

Here is the meaning of the words in the Moola Mantra:

Om—We are calling on the highest energy, of all there is

Sat—The formless

Chit—Consciousness of the Universe

Ananda—Pure love, bliss and joy

Parabrahma—The Supreme Creator

Purushothama—Who has incarnated in human form to help guide mankind

Paramatma—Who comes to me in my heart, and becomes my inner voice whenever I ask

Sri Bhagavati—The Divine Mother, the power aspect of Creation

Sametha—Together within

Sri Bhagavate—The Father of Creation, which is unchangeable and permanent

Namahal—thank you and acknowledge this presence in my life. I ask for your guidance at all times

When the proper words (especially Sanskrit) are used with the right music and rhythm, a most purifying effect can occur to the listener.

Moola Mantra CD and I AM Meditation CD

The word *om* comes from the Hindu religion, the *hu* sound (sounds like 'who') is from the Sufi religion; both sounds are intended to be chanted to help raise consciousness. Tibetans consider *kung* to be the great tone of nature. Shamans in many cultures use drums, rattles, flutes, and chants to heal the body and to gain access to the higher realms. Many aspects of sound are appreciated for their ability to affect changes in the body, mind, and spirit.

This mantra was recorded by me playing guitar and doing vocals, and with friends on bass and cello. Please take advantage of the mp3 version of this powerful healing mantra, available for FREE download from my web site: http://LifeseedCodes.com.

I AM Meditation

This guided meditation with music is a great primer for balancing the energy and invoking the light. You might choose to listen to the meditation with your participant, invoke the light, and clear the cords to set up a greater receptivity through focused breathing. It is clear from our observations of many people around the world, that a very deep-felt spirituality and a belief in the power of sound can help to re-shape and create positive change in our lives. It is also believed that certain mantras unwind the strings of karma. After a trip to Thailand to study mantra meditation and traditional Thai healing, I worked with a recorded mantra called Sai Sanyana. I always got the fullest night sleep and woke up feeling renewed after listening to that.

Listening with intent, such as for healing or meditation, can alter mood and, in effect, raise the energy vibration and improve our wellbeing. Make mindful selections of sound when balancing people.

A FREE mp3 download of the I AM Meditation is also available on the web site http://LifeseedCodes.com.

Emotions
Riding the Wave

It is inevitable that when you become proficient in this work you will have a person who, upon touching or possibly before, begins to cry and release. The best thing to do is to ride the wave by keeping as calm, compassionate, and present as possible. Support what is happening by simply being present or by simply keeping your hands on your client to communicate compassion.

We recently had an encounter where we had to hold a woman for a good ten to fifteen minutes until she got her story out. She had a reason to cry, she had a right to cry, and we did our best to support her. As it turns out, this person benefitted greatly from the brain balancing although she was in a lot of discomfort, she managed to have a positive response from the balancing. As of this writing, we have actually seen this woman a second time; she came with no tears and left in cheers. Balance is well suited for her. And she is morphing, body, mind, and spirit into a better state.

We do not have people's answers, but we do need to simply hold the energy or light for them. I like to explain to people that what I am going to do is the same process whether a person is four feet tall, five feet tall, six feet tall, eight years old or eighty years old, whether they are heavy or thin, happy, or sad.

It is best for them (when they can embrace the idea) that Alpha Brain Body Balancing is a type of assisted self-healing and that mindfulness is deeply appreciated. If a person on the table is receiving the work and they start talking, stop, step back and wait. They will get the message. Try not to work through talking. Just balance the energy and let nature do the rest.

Here is a bit of synchronicity, as I look up from the table at the library in Mount Vernon, Washington, I see a sign on a table...

                        Quiet
                        Study
                        Zone

Synchronization, hey?

Schumann Resonance

Feeling the Shift

Measurable electromagnetic waves in the earth's atmosphere, between the earth and the ionosphere, are what are referred to the Schumann Resonance. Physicist W.O. Schumann discovered the waves in 1952, describing them as the frequency produced by the earth's natural vibration.

This is observed as a pulse that is present in the particles moving in and out of the field, much like a body in respiration. For years, the resonance for these 'breaths' has been 7.83 Hz, but now it is spiking and ranging up to 5 or 10 and even 20 times that. As far back as one can imagine this field has been protecting all living things on earth. It has been doing this with a frequency of 7.83 Hz., a frequency primarily in the alpha and high theta range. This frequency has also been associated with a powerful range for hypnosis, suggestibility, healing, and meditation. Also, it has been reported that while this frequency is stimulated, people have increased levels of human growth hormone and cerebral blood flow levels.

For centuries yogis in India associated the 7.83 Hz as the frequency for OM, the "flow of pure sound." The body-mind really likes it. Our nervous system is influenced by the Earth's field and takes this signature into our body cells. Some say it is the keynote. Right now, the spikes are affecting us, but science is not sure what it is and, even if they knew, would they tell us? One thing is certain – the higher levels mean we must deal with more energy. For many people this means more stress, possibly transformation, or both. The spikes in the Shuman Resonance are like having the energy of the full moon last for days or even a week. It is intense. Some individuals say they know when it spikes because they get headaches. Emergency rooms see more false flag problems looking like heart attacks and even strokes during the intense times. Symptoms arise and then disappear quickly.

Gamma brain waves are twice as high as beta (stress) levels but are NOT associated with survival states. That is good if we can center this.

Many people suggest that we are going through a metamorphosis with the Earth, taking a huge evolutionary leap in consciousness.

I believe that we are at a turning point and that we have been in this turn for some time. Anyway, whether we are going to ascend, ascend, ascend, and then reach a new plateau or not is all yet to be seen. I am inclined to think that we are doing this. And I think you probably know what I am going to say here. Stay cool, stay calm, and stay balanced! You will enjoy the ride that much more.

> "When the earth's magnetic field environment is disturbed it can cause sleep disturbance, mental confusion, unusual lack of energy or a feeling of being on edge or overwhelmed for no apparent reason." [Source: the HeartMath website: heartmath.com]

Scientists are also investigating if changes in the earth's magnetic fields happen before natural catastrophes such as earthquakes, volcanic eruptions, and human initiated events such as riots, social unrest, and terror attacks.

Solar activity has not only had negative effects on society but has also been associated with positive collective growth and development such as architectural, artistic and scientific breakthroughs, as well as positive social change.

It has also been hypothesized that there may be a link between both human consciousness and the geomagnetic field: meaning the frequency that we emit, could well affect the geomagnetic field, as much as it affects us.

Relationship to the Heart

Of all our organs, it is the heart that generates the largest electromagnetic rhythm, which creates a field that is approximately 100 times stronger than that of the brain. With the right equipment the heart's electromagnetic field can be detected several feet from the body.

During quiet magnetic periods, Schumann resonance power (SRP) "appears to play an important role in synchronizing people's slow wave heart rhythms. The potential importance of these rhythms is currently unknown, but (eventually) it may be important to better understand human health and wellbeing." [Source: https://truththeory.com/2017/07/31/resonance-earths-geomagnetic-field-quadrupled-last-24-hours/

This is a big moment and only time will tell the effect it has on us collectively, but an understanding of an event can often help you to avert disaster. So, stay conscious of your actions.

Walk in Balance

Try to have contact with the Earth every day. Take your shoes off and visualize your body sending out a cord to the center of the planet. Imagine your cells coming into harmony and resonance with the planet.

Three different companies right now have systems at different price ranges that help balance available. One company is Centerpointe Research Institute with a system called Holosync. Another is SacredAcoustics.com (Karen Newell), and the third is the LifeflowProjectMeditation.com. Make your own best choice.

My preferred balance method is to use Brain Entrainment Systems from Lifeflow. Here is a sample below:

> LifeFlow® 7: Protects You from Harmful EMF Radiation
>
> "This track is specifically engineered to tune your brain to the 7.83Hz frequency, known as the Schumann Resonance. Scientists say our brains rely on this frequency to function properly ... and it has helped shape the evolution of life and our brains through eons of time.
>
> There is a problem though. ...The increasing exposure to EMF (Electromagnetic Field), radiation from electronics, cell phones, WiFi, computers, and more, blocks this natural rhythm of the earth. But, with the first level of the Theta Pack - LifeFlow® 7, you can bathe your mind in this nurturing 7.83Hz frequency combined with soothing sounds of forest rain. As a result, LifeFlow® 7..."

For daily information on the Schuman Resonance level go to:

https://www.disclosurenews.it/en/schumann-resonance-today-update/

Introduction to the Science of HUNA

Truly, the achievements of modern science are marvelous. The best way to learn the secrets of nature however is not by inventing instruments, but by improving the investigator himself.

Max Heindel,
The Rosicrucian Cosmo Conception,
Pacific Publishing Studio

"Let the Rain of Blessings Fall"

"Let that which is unknown become known"

Huna Prayers

"The ancient peoples of the pacific have handed down over a period of at least 14,000 years, certain concepts and practices which are in some ways more complete and comprehensive than the cumulative thought of modern physics, physicians and metaphysics." (Source: *Living in harmony*, Dr. Allan Lewis)

The above is a pretty bold statement, but I for one am inclined to believe it. Why? The kahunas (ones that knew the key) were able to demonstrate tremendous compliance with natural law. This gave them control (for lack of a better word) of things in their environment. In the bible we are told that man was given dominion over all things on the earth. The modern man's translation of this is that he can kill anything (except people) he wants to without digressing from the law or committing a mortal sin. A poor example of this is the current destruction of people burning the Amazon Rain Forest.

The Huna code of conduct is that there is only one sin, which is to do harm by hatred. Max Freedom Long is probably single-handedly the most important player in the resurrection of the Huna tradition which was outlawed shortly after the arrival of the Christian missionaries in Hawaii. When the Hawaiian midwives were no longer allowed to deliver the babies there were more deaths as a result, usually of the mothers. Max pointed out that while he lived in Hawaii there was never a single report of a shark attack. This is because the Hawaiians talked to the sharks as they interacted with all of nature and kept peace with the animals, plants, rocks, rivers, clouds, etc. They knew or understood and appreciated dominion through relatedness. Truth is stranger than fiction.

There are reports by Dr Bingham of Honolulu of kahunas resurrecting and resuscitating a drowned man roughly 16 hours after he was pulled from the water. The accounts of healing, fire walking, controlling waves, clouds and wind are enough to make you stand in amazement. They had integrated a profound appreciation of the earth and spirit, aloha, which means "in the presence of God." Perhaps they were (and still are) being guided, inspired and illuminated by invisible beings of light that speak the Language of Light. Some researchers say that there is a profound similarity between native or indigenous tribes all over the earth. Perhaps they share in the same spiritual ancestry or invisible teachers from these higher dimensions. If you study the oral tradition of the Huna you discover a profound reverence for the *amakua*, the higher self, and for the ancestors and the connection with those in spirit.

The following is from a reading from Edgar Cayce:

About angels and archangels:

> *"Yes, with the bringing into creation the manifested forms there came that which has been, is and ever will be, the spirit realm and its attributes-designated as angels and archangels. They are the Spiritual manifestation in the spirit world of those attributes that the developing forces accredit to the One Source, that may be seen in material planes through the influences that may aid in development of the mental and spiritual forces through an experience—or in the acquiring of knowledge that may aid in the intercourse one with another."*

I do not think that some new age person must prove that whoever had invented the wheel was channeling before we consider the possibility of life in other dimensions. It does appear that contact with these forces has been pivotal in man's understanding of his relationship with the creation, and with the Creator. Religions have been born out of our relationship with great men such as Jesus, Buddha, Krishna, Mohamed, Zoroaster, etc.

Direct contact with the forces of nature, such as the angelic realm, establishes deep and profound awarenesses in humanity about life, earth, spirit, nature which cannot be acquired in any other way; this is knowledge. Our argument has therefore been established here and now. If certain beings did not get the knowledge from the spirit world, from the realm of the masters and angels, where does it come from? Many people today speak of the visions of Christ. In fact, Serge King has offered us a fantastic example of this with his personal experience with the spiritual hierarchy in his book on Kahuna Healing.

It is with the greatest of pleasure that I begin sharing my enthusiasm and my connection with Huna energy and philosophy as a result of the profound synchronicity of being initiated into the work called Spirit Touch Healing (Kofutu), an aspect of Huna Kane. This particular aspect of Huna involves a hands-on process with the use of symbols for the integration of the High Self, also called *amaukua*. The symbols work as activating energies that connect us to the High Self. Somehow, I wound up at the home of a powerful kahuna on one of my trips to Florida. I was sharing and teaching a Brain Body Balancing technique to a contact there. After working on three people, I started teaching them how we balance and synchronize the left/right hemispheres of the brain and the results on strength, leg length and clearing by using this technique. Our hostess Deb insisted that she teach me her work and gave me the symbols to facilitate the link. I was amazed and blessed.

Call it what you will, but now we are able to lay on our hands and produce measurable, testable results with presence or energy. We can measure leg length, arm strength and determine that the brain is in beta, switched on in emergency for no reason. Through thought, intention and the use of a symbol held in consciousness, in a matter of six breaths we can establish balance.

The following is a quote from *The Sacred Power of Huna* by Rima Morrell.

> *"As we have seen, the application of Huna is based on understanding of the principal of attraction that underlies all of existence and provides the means for the various powerful aspects of Hawaiian shamanism, we attract things by way of the mana-force we project onto the world through our three minds: the superconscious, conscious, and subconscious. The mana sticks to the aka,(etheric) the substances of which all things are made. Getting the results we want, depends on the alignment of the three minds and the direction of consciousness."*

Mana is life force both magnetic and electric. We absorb it from the food that we eat and the air that we breathe. Slow conscious breathing is a way to accumulate an extra amount of energy or mana, which is then used for special intent, prayer and purpose.

I began to explore the concept of the trinity of lower, middle and higher self by following an exercise that is suggested in *The Secret Science at Work* by Max Freedom

Long, of talking to the Lower Self as if it was MY job to help this little fellow evolve, and that we had better be on good terms about it. In getting acquainted with the Lower Self we realize its unique qualities and capacities. This way of looking at our unique organization as the trinity of being has been monumental for us in our study group. The following will bring clarity to the idea of the trinity. I will start at the bottom and work our way to the Superconscious, or High self.

Yourself as the Trinity

The three selves in the Huna tradition are considered as follows: Aumakua, the Higher Self or superconsciousness, our perfect self. Also called our "I AM Presence."

The Middle Self, Uhane, which is comprised of our conscious mind, personal identity, and rational mind.

The Lower Self: Unihipili, is our subconscious mind, home to our memory and emotions. Our connection to our higher aspects demands we keep a clean and open dialogue going with this aspect of self.

We will begin here from the basic spirit or low self and work up to the higher. I have begun to think of this aspect as the inheritance from our mother, Earth. Below are some of the qualities, conditions, and activities.

The Lower Self

1. The Lower or Basic Self is a separate and conscious entity. (Your conscious middle mind can and must make contact with it.)
2. It is a servant of the upper selves and is attached to the middle or conscious self. It can only deduct from information stored within itself, like a filing system.
3. The Lower Self has control of ALL processes of the body, memory, and all function except for the voluntary muscles.
4. It is the seat of the emotions. It is a powerhouse and IT MUST BE ENGAGED TO CONTACT THE HIGH SELF.
5. The Lower Self manufactures all the vital forces, or mana, to be used by the three selves. When we are effective in attraction or healing it is because we

have charged the Low Self with mana and sent it to the High Self to carry on our request for us.

6. The Lower Self receives all sensory impressions and relays them to the conscious or middle mind.
7. The Low Self has perfect memory and responds to requests of the middle mind or spirit.
8. The Low Self or spirit is subject to suggestion and hypnosis, it can be redirected, transformed. It can let go and release trauma, programs, etc.
9. The Lower Self or spirit may hold unrationalized ideas in its aka body as memory clusters-imprints-impressions-engrams that do not serve the evolving being. The work of "Clearing your Life" involves the discovery and dissolution of any limited programs or data and downloading positive programming. This is a moment to moment process of watching your thoughts and only giving energy or mana to the ones you would see manifest. In other words, if a memory comes up you can use Ho'oponopono to clear with. This is discussed fully in the following essay, an "Introduction to Ho'oponopono."

Positive reprogramming through conscious dialoging is the ongoing work of Selves (three in one) mastery. YOU must liberate the subconscious or basic or low self by speaking your wisdom to this childlike aspect of yourself and free it from all complexes so THAT IT WILL PASS ALONG YOUR PRAYERS TO THE HIGH SELF.

You must therefore tell your basic self that it is forgiven, cleansed, and greatly loved. Tell it every day!

Since communication with the High Self is not possible without the assistance of the Low Self, we have been placed in a most deliberate and universal dynamic of extending to support an aspect of being as we would have our High Self support us. As they say in Hermetic philosophy "As above so below, for the fulfillment of the one thing," and in the Golden Rule "Do unto others as you would have them do unto you," only this time, first, do it unto yourself.

The Lower Self form of mentation is rather simple and limited, but you could not run the machinery of the body without it. The Middle Self has evolved to a place where its reasoning powers are vastly superior. The Higher Self transcends both memory and reason and is beyond comprehension in its full nature. Some believe that the High Self is the God within and connected to all of life. It is my goal here to offer a basic outline of the three minds or spirit unity, offer reasons to keep in alignment, and instruction to facilitate this link. The Brain Body Balance hands-on work is a dynamic example of High Self-integration. Meditation, prayer and invocation clearly facilitate this unity and are the practice of all enlightened men and women.

Now, this is an important point to consider: In making a prayer to manifest anything, the Low Self contacts the High Self by means of the aka cord, done through the breath and intention, which it activates and sends along to the High Self for its use. Your High Self will visit the body, but for most untrained persons, will reside outside and above attached by the aka cord. The magic and power of the shaman/kahuna results from this alignment, integration of the three minds (spirits) and the ability to accumulate and direct mana/energy drawn in on the breath. The aka cord is invisible etheric substance that connects the selves or brains, and also persons to persons.

The way to your Source/Creator/God is through the High Self. The way to the High Self is through the LOW Self. This is a distinction that is not practical in modern religious thought. In modern religious systems of the western culture, too much emphasis is given to the conscious process of the Middle Self. In Eastern thought the emphasis is quite the reverse. "No Mind, Only the Self" is a statement of liberation or enlightenment. The West has been slow to realize integration of this philosophy. Understanding and applying the concept and psychology of the Huna, of the Trinity of Being, is clearly one of the most rational, universal, scientific processes that is both simple and practical and can be applied by persons of any faith. It is like the equivalent of water in your diet.

Engaging the Low Self

At first the idea of having an aspect within and of talking to the Low Self seemed strange to me. I tried it anyway. This involves talking to yourself as if you had a smaller younger self inside you that had the controls of your biological organism. The more I worked with this idea the clearer things became for me. I have been doing High Self-intuitive dowsing for years. Now, I was linking with the body, Low Self, and being able to begin to unravel some of my blocks to joy, success and fulfillment.

Just a few weeks after I engaged with this discipline my dowsing instructor, Carole Conlon, reorganized her system. She is now working with the concept of a personal trinity of Ego, Soul and Self and to harmonize this triad before we do our clearing work. We are coming up with better results. We had both come to the new way of working from different angles or sources. It is interesting to note that when we dowsed for the percentage of harmony, agreement, and cooperation that I had with my ego, soul and spirit I was functioning at a higher percentage than most. This will vary in humans. This was a great confirmation for the three-mind/spirit concept, the Low Self-alignment, as well as the power of the High Self alignment process.

It is interesting to me that the trinity is also mentioned in that timeless classic *The Impersonal Life*. It should also be noted that the appreciation of the subconscious and superconscious pre-dated our modern discovery as attributed to Freud and Jung. As of today, June 12, 2019, we have never tested anyone before Brain Body Balance activation at over 65% and we have worked with individuals who have tested as low as 15% integration of body-mind-spirit. No wonder the culture is in the doghouse. With all the emphasis on religion and the macrocosm, we have failed to keep our houses in order, the microcosm, and the Trinity.

Working with the subconscious mind (Lower Self) allows one to retrain it in a positive way by removing negative ego programming that has been incorrectly placed there over the years by television, teachers, siblings, parents, and events. The lower mind wants to be perfect in function and align with the rational middle mind. Every thought produces a chemical response in the body, which is either acid or alkaline. With proper guidance it is possible to take even the worst memory and defuse it. Initially, we work with forgiveness to open the life path or way of communication.

In the LifeWeaving Dowsing method, we work with breath energy such as sending compassion into our organs, chakras, or subtle bodies to liberate blocks, interference, and intrusions, and then breathe the White Light to redeem, remove, replace and recharge these areas. We are learning to direct a channel of exact frequencies of light and sound and essence. In our case, we are working with pendulums and dowsing charts, however; it is not necessary to dowse to begin to "Clear your Life."

It is very helpful to understand that unless you positively reprogram the Lower Self and begin aligning with Spirit or High Self, you cannot create a new future. Some say bad habits do die-hard. Thank God we have been given an easier way to become powerfully effective in clearing, cleaning, and moving on.

It is unfortunate that, as children at home, we learn whom, how and when to love and who to hate. It is fortunate when we can discover the ageless wisdom teachings such as Huna, which can help us re-establish our humanity and consider the possibility of enlightened values. It is mainly the subconscious mind that holds the sin, guilt and fear, hates and grudges. Mistakes mean to try over or take again. We learn in the Huna philosophy the profound and ONE simple commandment that is to "harm no one with hate." There is no mortal sin in missing a meeting or falling short as a human being in any area. At least short of harming with hate which can also be forgiven, one would make amends for his or her ways and errors, forgive and be forgiven and be done with it. When you forgive you look past and release your cords (aka) so that your energy is free of interference. The Ho'oponopono process was developed for engaging the forgiveness principle and cultivated in each individual as well as in the circle of acquaintances, friends, and family. We will explain this process in greater detail further on in the essay. Also, see the Re-Set Exercise, from my book "*I AM Presence*" in the appendix.

Because of the guilt-ridden imprints we have received from our culture and environment we continue to be punished by the subconscious mind. Let us now begin a process of restoration and renewal by contacting the Lower Self, have a meeting in kindness and truth, in forgiveness and peace, and turn a corner towards more personal joy and satisfaction.

If everything that you have learned about yourself is from the outside, then it is time to start peeling away the layers like an onion and find out something for yourself, the real and true you.

The following is a simple exercise to bring the conscious mind and subconscious mind into greater rapport. If you have a study partner you can ask for assistance and have them read this to you.

We have a *free* beautiful recording of this breathing meditation done by Karin Couture. Please contact me at http://LifeSeedCodes.com and I will send you the file by email.

Opening to Dialog with the Low Self

(Lie down or sit in a comfortable position.)

> Become aware of your breath.
>
> Give your body the suggestion to relax.
>
> Begin relaxing the feet, breathe into the feet, and breathe into the feet,
>
> Now breathe into your legs and breathe into your legs.
>
> Let them relax, feel them relax.
>
> Now breathe into your hips and stomach, breathe into your hips and stomach.

Let them relax, feel them relax.

Now relax the center of your body, relax the center of your body.

Let it relax, feel it relax.

Be still and relax; each breath takes you deeper into a state of perfect relaxation.

Be still and relax; each breath takes you deeper into a state of perfect relaxation.

Now breathe into your chest and back, breathe into your chest and back.

Now breathe into your chest and back, breathe into your chest and back.

Let them relax, feel them relax.

Now breathe into your shoulders, breathe into your arms and hands.

Now breathe into your shoulders, breathe into your arms and hands.

Let them relax, feel them relax.

Breathe into your neck and head, breathe into your neck and head.

Let them relax, feel them relax.

My nervous system is relaxing,

I AM relaxing, I AM Still,

I AM in the Silence. . . (Pause)

I AM Relaxing, I AM Still,

I AM in the Silence.

Congratulations! You have just deepened the relationship of the Lower Self or subconscious, and the Middle Self or conscious mind. Whether you are a beginner or a seasoned meditator, it does not matter. Each time you bring the conscious mind in the neighborhood of the subconscious, you work on the relationship. Rather than just lying down and relaxing, you work each body part and facilitate greater unity. Once you become comfortable with this part of the work you can go on and talk with the subconscious. Make it good! Put your heart into it.

Here is a Statement Which can Begin the Healing:

My dear and wonderful subconscious mind, My Low Self
Thank you for running my body and maintaining my memory so well for me.
I am so fortunate to have you in my life.
I am so fortunate to have you in my life.
I am so fortunate to have you in my life.
Now, I wish to offer apologies to you for having handled things in the past, in ways that might have compromised our positive alignment one to another.

I am truly sorry if I have offended you in any way or caused you to hurt at any time. I was young and did not understand my value system at the time.
I will forgive you now and ask for your forgiveness for any and all wrongs of the past.

I wish to extend my gratitude to you.
I wish to extend my gratitude to you.
I wish to extend my gratitude to you.

I will pray to God that I might begin to understand the gift of life, the gift of my freedom and begin charging you, my subconscious with more mana, love, and overall positive energy.

I will pray to God that I might begin to understand the gift of life, the gift of my freedom and begin charging you, my subconscious, with more mana, love, and overall positive energy.
I will pray to God that I might begin to understand the gift of life, the gift of my freedom and begin charging you, my subconscious with more mana, love, and overall positive energy.

I will open myself to the guidance from positive centered people and from my High Self and my High Self committee to lead me on the path of right justice, prosperity, and peace.

I here and now commit to a life filled with love, compassion, harmony, and personal growth.

I here and now commit to a life filled with love, compassion, harmony, and personal growth.
I here and now commit to a life filled with love, compassion, harmony, and personal growth.

Now Breathe in Cooperation and breathe out Cooperation.
Now Breathe in Cooperation and breathe out Cooperation.
Now Breathe in Cooperation and breathe out Cooperation.

Now breathe in Empathy and Breathe out Empathy.
Now breathe in Empathy and Breathe out Empathy.
Now breathe in Empathy and Breathe out Empathy.

Now breathe in Reconciliation and Breathe out Reconciliation.
Now breathe in Reconciliation and Breathe out Reconciliation.
Now breathe in Reconciliation and Breathe out Reconciliation.

Now breathe in Unity and Breathe out Unity.
Now breathe in Unity and Breathe out Unity.
Now breathe in Unity and Breathe out Unity.

Now each day that you practice conscious breathing you are establishing your connection with your Low Self and its innate wisdom.

Breathe Awareness in and Breathe awareness out.
Breathe Awareness in and Breathe awareness out.
Breathe Awareness in and Breathe awareness out.

I AM here to open myself, align my Self and Unify.
I AM here to open myself, align my Self and Unify.
I AM here to open myself, align my Self and Unify.

I call forth now in this moment the Sacred Trinity.
I call forth now in this moment the Sacred Trinity.
I call forth now in this moment the Sacred Trinity.

I commit at this moment to keep the lines of communication open.
I commit at this moment to keep the lines of communication open.
I commit at this moment to keep the lines of communication open.

So that I will fulfill on my responsibilities, obligations, and duties.
So that I will fulfill on my responsibilities, obligations, and duties.
So that I will fulfill on my responsibilities, obligations, and duties.

And Arise in Light, Love and Consciousness
And Arise in Light, Love and Consciousness
And Arise in Light, Love and Consciousness

Now, let your body completely relax, close your eyes, and feel into a pleasant sensation of harmony and well-being.
Allow yourself a few more moments to council within Your Self.

It is important to engage these practices when you are in the proper mood. These are sacred moments that you have self to self. Practice, practice and then practice some more. In martial arts training they say that if you want to move fast to practice moving slow. If you want to move like lightening, then practice standing still. Practice moving into the silence and begin to move like lightening in your desired areas of participation. Be Still and Know. Be Still and Breathe Mana into the Lower Self. Send out an aka cord and connect to the High Self. Now energize the High Self and send your prayer image. Relax!

Know that the subconscious is your friend. It wishes to be absolutely straight with you, absolutely for you. Make peace and you will have peace. As John Lennon said, "and in the end, the love you take is equal to the love you make."

Then you will hear the still, small voice of the High Self coming through the Low Self because the way is clearing for you. No Worry! No Blame! No Problem, only forgiveness! It is through the Low Self that we connect to the High Self. Some say, and I quote "There is no other way to do it." Developing this three-way communication is one of the main aims of study for those (kahunas) who would be sorcerers, people connected to their source. Put yourself into the silence when you want to talk to the Low Self and when you establish rapport you will notice an immediate response. Your negative self-talk can truly transform to powerful positive self-unfolding.

Do this instead: I love you, I am sorry, please forgive me, Thank you.

Prayer in Huna Philosophy

Once we have cultivated the ability to enter the silence we can begin to bring into harmony, agreement, and cooperation the connection of the Low Self to the Middle, we can then begin to charge up the Low Self with the mana to send it to the High Self so that results may be obtained. I grew up in the Catholic school system and had this religion forced upon my psyche. My understanding of prayer was something you did before a game or report card. You prayed that you would be kept safe from the beatings, which might come if you disappointed the father with bad scores. My life was all about points. Prayer was also something we did after confession as a penance. I was probably left with different points of view and purposes as a result. Prayer, as I appreciate it today, is something more congruent. I realize that the ability to converse with the father/mother within is a rare privilege and activity. It is a privilege that all beings can enjoy and, in fact, is heralded by some as being the most significant quality of being human. Walter Russell, in his groundbreaking home study course on Natural Science and Philosophy, dedicated his whole second lesson to the concept of prayer. Meditation was his first lesson. In the Huna philosophy there is one specific fact of prayer technique and that is that ALL THREE of the SELVES have their parts to play. If any one of the parts is missing the operation is useless.

In order for a prayer formula to succeed in Huna philosophy, it has to be defined by the middle mind, the outer or personal being, and then passed to the Low Self who energizes it with mana and passes it on to the High Self. It is necessary to have developed a telepathic relationship between the Low and High Selves or else the attempts of the Person (Middle Self) almost always result in failure. Max Freedom Long says in his book, *The Secret Science at Work*, that "The tragedy of the twenty centuries that have elapsed since the time of Christ and his teaching, is that this part of the secret was lost, that men failed to retain the knowledge of what prayer was, and how to use it."

If man is to be a co-creator and prayer is the enzyme that produces the activation and flow from the invisible world of energy/possibility to the physical world of matter/form, it is absolutely required that we come to an appreciation of the process as soon as possible, and as powerfully as possible. It may be true that this congruency is what we must become balanced in, for all our affairs require it. I notice with friends that I believe to be very "spiritual," a distinct lack of appreciation for the power of prayer, and a certain embarrassment about it. I don't get it. I love to pray! I sense that we are lost as a people and we must establish our connection with the Creator now and put an end to our troubles with one another. In fact, by simply bringing the ego, soul and self into harmony we out picture a different possibility and produce a different outcome.

When I counsel people with the LifeWeaving process, I ask spirit to help me clear them and establish rapport. When we return to the issues after clearing there is often a whole new perspective and new possibilities arise. Our issues are opportunities in disguise.

As a Doctor of Divinity and minister, I have performed over 1,000 ceremonies, done healings and counseled many people. I have done teacher training in Bija Meditation here in the Northwest and made trips for initiation to the Far East. I have had the good fortune of meeting and studying with many great teachers. It was not until I was reacquainted with HUNA, and again came to appreciate the necessity of "Clearing Your Life" that I understood why so many healers and teachers fail. They are trying to transcend and to the degree that they overlooked the concept of the healthy triad of Low, Middle and High Self, they were unable to succeed. A Mantra or technique can take you into new dimensions of possibility, but what is required to graduate the lessons of this planet and move on to new horizons is to have our acts together on *all* Levels, physically, mentally, emotionally, and spiritually. Being congruent as a being of light, as a co-creator is your birthright; claim it, develop it and unfold the mastery that is yours to express. It is a gift from your Source. It is a gift only when it is opened.

The Sacred Trinity

Ever notice the pictures of the masters and saints and just how beautiful they usually are. Most pictures of the master Jesus depict him as an attractive being. If you have ever seen the I AM material with pictures of Saint Germain and others, and even the statues of the Buddha and Quan Yin, one quality they all share is a type of beauty that radiates from inside out. The opposite is also true. Imbalance stands out just as well as a sense of balance. The sacred trinity of selves is a possibility for all beings, but as you can notice, humanity likes to gravitate towards chaos, has a curiosity for the goofy, and has tendencies to magnetize the problem reality. If you do not believe me, just watch the news, and notice where the attention is being placed.

How can we create an ongoing interest in the profound, the beautiful and the wonderful? Some are already there in our lives. Some have set the intention to engage this more and more. Others still have not got a clue. I heard a woman say (I will not quote) that a harsh and brutal punishment should be enacted upon men that abuse women, children, etc. Understanding that the High Self is fully equipped with compassion and understanding for us, I am thinking that just the projection of these thoughts would cause an individual holding these thoughts to fragment, causing the High Self to move away. The High Self will not be a party to any foul play, no way. If a person acts out any violence then the Low Self becomes fearful of retribution, becomes guilt-ridden and disassociates itself. Fragmentation is the result, and it shows up in people's bodies as well as their lives. Practicing the law of forgiveness, for others, and ourselves will produce more unity and lightness of spirit.

There are three things that prevent the Low Self from communicating with the High Self and establishing a Unity of Being. The first thing is guilt. The second thing is outside influences such as entity attachment. The third thing is beliefs. Our memories are shaped by our beliefs. Keeping an open mind is an invaluable thing. Jesus said that in order to enter the kingdom of God, we must become as little children.

Maintenance is the needed magic for the High Self and the basic self; dialog with them often and you will notice great change and development in all areas of your life and especially in your relationships. The world gravitates towards people in balance. Keep your priorities right. Staying in balance is an important way to keep on keeping on the path of return, the path for fulfillment in the righteous sense.

Communicate with yourself and love yourself and the world is a better place. The positive alignment of the three brains or three spirits brings a sense of unity, balance, and sacredness to life. How do we stay there? Take care of all the small details. Check in every day to see if the triad of High Self, Middle Self and Low Self are in harmony, cooperation, and agreement. Balance the trinity of the ego, self and soul and endeavor to keep it balanced.

The Middle Self

There are two types of knowledge in the world, cultural is one of them, and sacred knowledge is the other.

The conscious mind is a great servant when it is aligned with the Higher Self through the agency of the Low Self, a wonderful servant, but a terrible boss.

The middleman, called *lono* or conscious mind as it is referred to in modern psychology, is the analytical aspect of being. It is this aspect that coordinates, integrates, assesses, and determines our course of action in the world. This aspect of being is influenced by our environment, education and forms, attitudes, beliefs, and opinions. It can be organized around the idea that we are evolving beings in an evolving universe. Or it can be a protector of tradition, prejudiced and closed off to any degree, bound by the sensory mechanisms of the body and senses. I suspect that most of us fall somewhere in the center with our philosophy. I was told by an Indian Swami "that until we reach enlightenment all that the mind does is project." Projection is a function of the subconscious.

Since the conscious mind is the accepter or rejecter of our reality, we make it all up anyway. Our perception is our god, and a very, very small one at that. Meditation allows us to become still and know. We enter the silence and re-emerge as greater possibilities for participation, for life. We must engage The UNITY OF BEING to change, adapt and grow. Our beliefs are more important than anything because they shape our memories. Some minds are more capable of withstanding the challenges of growth and maturity. Life happens and often it is a complex event, and yet some minds are more capable of rolling with it. Many a successful soul has never taken a problem or obstacle personally. They move towards their desired goals undaunted, powerfully, and each obstacle makes them stronger. Others are afraid of failure in life. They might not even try. Again, most of us are perhaps somewhere in the middle. While often people will take a miracle (such as love) and make it mundane, the whole purpose of applying Huna or miracle consciousness, or the Cosmic Christ Consciousness Vibration to life is to turn the mundane back into the sacred, where it belongs.

The conscious mind as the middleman between the High Self and the Low Self works optimally only when the lines of communication are open, period. If we have filled the subconscious/lower self/mind with prejudice, pride and problems stemming from guilt or blame, then contact with the High Self is compromised, guidance is not received. It may be flowing to us, but not necessarily received by us. Some venture to say that the conscious mind does not reincarnate but is discarded at death. The surface self is just the reflection in the mirror of consciousness. The High Self collects all the love, experience and growth that has been generated in each life and the associated values from the works of balance, beauty, and originality, and moves on into the higher realm. The Lower aspect, which has worked ceaselessly for purpose and the pleasures of life moves on to its happy resting ground only to redefine, redevelop and redirect itself into the life process again, until it ascends to the level of the Higher Self.

One day, we will understand with certainty the origin, activity and culmination or fulfillment of the selves, but for now you can see the sometimes-profound results that occur by simply having them aligned. One thing that stands out for certain is that one can flow with changes much easier when the triad of selves is balanced. So, talk to God often and listen in the stillness of meditation. Talk to the body when breathing mana and express your gratitude for its support, sustenance, and service to you.

Simply put, the power that is beating your own heart right now is the great ONE power of Universe, God. This very breath that you breathe is your connection to your Source, but only if you can own this idea. There is no need of salvation, really, except from yourself. In living and thinking and being, all is a matter of perception. You are continually in motion, as an evolving being in an evolving universe you will continually make course corrections. The Huna is a cosmic compass directing you onward and upward. Use it if you dare. Use it if you will. Use it through Intention. Use the power of the silence, the breath and mana force, and the Sacred Trinity to gain knowledge of the magnificent universe of YOU. In other words, bless You, empower You, keep You, discover You and to your own Self be true.

The Super Conscious Mind

The Amakua refers to the High Self in Huna philosophy. It is considered the absolute loving utterly trustworthy grand parental self. It is the mind of the Buddha in the East. It is the music from the flute of Krishna. It is the heart of the living Christ, the Sky Mind of the Tibetans, the spark of God of the existentialists. Every culture has an idea and name, and all agree. It is the Essence of Life and it is within us, and it is the source of revelation for us. Our lives are a flow of consciousness upon matter, into the living fabric of light and life. Without the agency of the High Self we would be reduced to automatons in fixed orbits and fixed habits. Life would be truly empty and meaningless.

The High Self or super conscious mind is said to reside in the energy field, and some say it is the causal body, or our personal angel. It will enter our lives for guidance from time to time only for positive purposes. It does not have human values. It resides in a permanent state of balance. And this balance is a state of love, compassion, realized self-existence, fulfillment, and oneness. It is beyond the concept of the conscious mind, yet we can see its effect like wind upon the water. We can attract and gather to ourselves the energy and guidance of the God within, irrespective of race, color, creed or credentials. It is considered the great equalizer of life; each person has the same access to the God within.

Cosmic Principals According to Huna

Everything is a manifestation of Divine Energy. There is but One Source.
This Source is above and beyond Name and Form, yet symbolized as I-A-O.

I   Represents that creative act by which that which is perfect, manifests that which is perfect, as creator of all perfection, from nothing to now a thing, from nowhere to now here.

A   Represents the radiation and flow of substance or energy and is not at all limited to expression in this physical dimension. The great power of the sun anchors space/time, yet humanity comes from beyond, as do our guardians of spirit. We entered into this life stream as sparks of light.

In order to manifest in the physical, we needed to be housed or covered, therefore we were given dust or clay bodies. Spirit (sun or breath) then entered in. Thus arose duality.

> Our responsibility is also our freedom which is twofold: to honor and enjoy nature, to consciously realize our true Spiritual nature.
>
> All life forms have guidance and essence in spirit. We are not alone in the universe and we must align ourselves with the guidance and inspiration flowing to us from spirit for our growth and evolution.
>
> We have been guided by, educated by, nourished by these beings of light since the fall of man, since our consent to play the polarity game.
>
> In the physical, we always function with two options in consciousness. We can synchronize and balance the opposites and be awake. Or we can go into duality, darkness, and ignorance.

O   Represents the Sacred Name, the goal, the omnipresent, omnipotent, omniscient, the All That Is.

A note to mention here is that a great part of science and technology is now going to energize the war machine, pharmaceutical development, and industry that has negative impact on both human development as well as the environment. We have form without substance, duality, and an imminent danger associated with technology; those forms function without heart/substance/spirit.

It is therefore the responsibility of those who would be free to continue to evolve and complete our Earth studies and lessons; to vibrate into our experience those people, places, and things that further that action and accomplishment. The balance is, however, that you must allow those beings who are bent on destructive habits to do their own thing, because this is a free will zone.

Developing Personal Power

The bible says that all things flow from above, downward, and from inside out. The awareness of the breath and focusing of an idea, inspiration, or intention, then sending it to the Low Self to relay on to the High Self, is the pivotal process in developing personal power. Once you learn it, it is like walking and chewing gum at the same time. Hold your intention, breathe, and then contact the bodies (physical, subtle) and release. The breath energizes your prayer. Below is a rough outline of how the Ha Rite Ritual has been handed down over the centuries. Of course, the principles of wellbeing must become second nature to us. To *re-spect* means to look again. Only by anchoring the principles for harmony and balance can we expect to have the personal power to succeed. Below are listed the important ideas.

1. Everything starts with you. You co-create your own reality. Life itself is empty and meaningless. People are meaning-making machines.
2. Energy follows thought so you will attract what you think upon or about.
3. The buck stops with you and you are responsible for your experience, all of it.
4. You are an attractor in a universe of attraction. Think positive and have positive. The opposite is also true.
5. All thought is creative on some level. Be Still and Know Often.
6. Change the cause and you will change the effect.
7. With God all things are possible. With You all things are possible. Believe and receive, doubt and do without.
8. Now is the only time you have. Be here now!
9. Energy flows where attention goes.

10. There is no such thing as an accident. The universe is a well-oiled machine.
11. You are equipped with an internal guidance system that works in miraculous ways, but only with the on switch turned on.

The HA Rite Ritual

The word used to describe the white man in the Hawaiian Islands was haole, 'one who has no breath.' They were observed in their prayer ritual as muttering a few sentences with a bowed head and then being done with it. The celebration, the connection was missing. Anyone who knew the aloha spirit knew that this technique (the breath) was a way to gather to themselves a supply of universal life force energy from the One Source for use in their prayers. Their understanding and beliefs were that unless you charge the prayer with enough mana and send it along to the High Self, then results were not obtained.

The following is an exercise for doing the process. It might be studied in a group or with one person facilitating; however, one person can read through a few times and then do it. The affirmations may be added or omitted depending on one's own preferences. After you understand the principle it can be personalized by you and done and enjoyed often. Pray for Peace. Pray for Progress for Humanity.

There are four specific steps in a power or prayer process.

Step One - Enter into the Silence and begin conscious breathing while commanding the Low Self to produce an extra supply of mana. Do as many breaths as you feel comfortable with. The Yogis in India use the same principal and they might breathe prana for hours. The important thing is to initiate a psycho/physical shift and move away from normal consciousness towards the domain of miracles. When I work, I almost always feel a noticeable sense of my crown chakra tingling, my heart chakra expanding and my solar plexus chakra vibrating into my whole body. I like to think of it as my sacred trinity meeting to counsel with one another, with good vibes. It is powerful to exercise the gift of life, thinking, asking, seeking and knocking on the door. Watch and it will open for you.

Affirmation: *In the Divine name of God, I request my Low Self to charge up with mana. In the name of my High Self within me, I cleanse this unit of all negativity so that I may be a perfect vessel for the I AM presence within.*

Step Two - Call out to the Higher Self through the Low Self or subconscious for contact. You have a prayer, a request, or an intention that will bring into your life a new pattern or matrix or design of being, or form and creation. You must dial in, make the contact. This is the difference between wishful thinking and making a wish.

Affirmation: *My subconscious and I are now in harmony and balance. We invite you, oh Higher Self, to come all the way down and receive this new pattern, this prayer for my life.*

Step Three - Visualize the request and FEEL contact with the presence of the High Self. A picture is worth a thousand words.

Affirmation: *This is the image that I send with mana and love and appreciation for you. Bring this new pattern into life, so be it.*

Step Four - Say your prayer while continuing to breathe and send mana. Some persons feel comfortable by raising the palm of their hands next to the ears and feel the energy flow. Visualize a fountain of energy moving to the Higher Self, powerfully energizing the request and process. You may choose to repeat your prayer a few more times up to as many as four.

Affirmation: *To you my Higher Self, I send you mana for as a gift of gratitude and so that you may water the seeds we have planted and bring them to reality in right timing.*

Step Five – Completion: Say "This as a prayer takes flight, let the rain of blessings fall." This is a prayer that has been utilized and handed down by the Kahunas for ages. You might like to sit quietly for a few moments continuing to be aware of the breathing and just enjoy any sensations that come over you. There may be gentle whispers from spirit.

Release yourself slowly from the silence and let the energy modulate to normal waking state and energy flow. It is important to appreciate the shifts into and out of this trance-like state to receive the most benefit. If you have already been into meditation or self-hypnosis, you will have already gone over the territory and become familiar with brain states and shifting from beta (high thought count) to alpha and theta states.

As you can see, the work of self-transformation is specific and direct. The fact that this has been taught by wisdom workers for thousands of years, by many different names, affirms the reality that as a people we are being led by our forces that be.

The still small voice that is within each and every one of us can be heard if the right conditions are met, and then many a miracle was, is and will be, to follow.

Ho'oponopono

There is a legendary story of a man known as Dr.Ihaleakala Hew Len, who cured every patient in the criminally insane ward of a Hawaiian State Hospital — without ever seeing a single patient.

Now I AM curious about this, how about you?

> *"For the rest of my life I want to reflect on what Light is."*
> Albert Einstein

> What if every atom in the universe responded to the observer?
> Please be careful how you look there!

The 'observer effect' is the fact that simply observing a situation or phenomenon necessarily changes that phenomenon.

Water and its Response to Frequency

The human body, over 70% water, is receptive to our thoughts, energies, frequencies and emotions in its crystalline and molecular levels. The pictures of the total of our experiences are playing out in our bodies and keeping our history - like a library holds books, videos and DVD's. If we empty the history we can fill up with the mystery of life's forces, energies, light and spontaneity.

> *"We are the sum total of our experiences, which is to say that we are burdened by our pasts. When we experience stress or fear in our lives, if we would look carefully, we would find that the cause is actually a memory. It is the emotions that are tied to these memories that affect us now. The subconscious associates an action or person in the present with something that happened in the past. When this occurs, emotions are activated, and stress is produced."*
>
> Morrnah Nalamaku Simeona

The two most powerful words to affect the crystalline structures of the water content of your body are love and gratitude, love and gratitude. So, you may repeat this mantra/affirmation, "I love you, I'm sorry, please forgive me, thank you", over and over and over to shift your inner and crystalline matrix in the body/mind.

To Raise Your Vibration, You Let Go

Heal your life and release negativity when you realize that you do not need to energize, focus on and otherwise validate stuff, people, places and things.

Have a reconciliation, forgiveness and neutralization of data, release of the karma, patterns, and thought materials through a consciousness transformation formula.

Have a positive effect on the field of relationships by staying home in the Self and generating a wholesome healing forgiving thankful loving frequency, which does the cleaning. Who or what does the cleaning? Who knows? Who cares? It is magic and beyond the conscious mental process. It restores a balance.

Being effective and flexible in ways and directions of application means Ho'oponopono becomes mental floss that turns misery into mastery.

- Step One: Pause and then breathe awareness, because data equals beta. Beta is a stress frequency. Beta is a great frequency for weightlifting, downhill skiing, running, but not effective for releasing and slowing down. Breathe in awareness.

- Step Two: Replace data with mindfulness by repetition of the formula.

    Data defined: data is the mind stream of thoughts, judgments, and aggravations that are keeping us distracted from living powerful and fulfilling lives.

    The Formula: I love you, I'm sorry, please forgive me, thank you. (In any order)

    It is not personal. There is no subject. You don't hurl pono at someone, place or thing. You let go!

    Some Ho'oponopono people will tell you to focus on the problem or person and perhaps to even state the name. At this moment I disagree with that process. Why is that? Because people love drama and whatever you put your attention on seems to grow. Generating a FREQUENCY of healing, of loving, of forgiving and gratitude does not require a story, period.

- Step Three: Check and see if you really mean it. If you don't, or can't, mean it universally then just do this for yourself. Thank you, that is sufficient. Our self-contractions open gradually, so be gentle with thyself and things will powerfully transform.

Remember that forgiveness is not about making someone guilty and then giving them a get out of jail free card. It is always only about zero. And zero has no memory. The presence is always in "Now." Being in the stream of consciousness with the Higher Self happens when present time awareness is where our attention is.

Does memory happen? Absolutely! It comes up for cleaning!

Do the cleaning, do the cleaning, and do the cleaning.

Because when the subconscious mind is absolutely sure that your aim is a drama free state, it will do the cleaning for you!

An Ancient Indian Mantra Like Ho'oponopono

Lokah Samastah Sukhino Bhavantu
Ancient Mantra

Meaning: May I radiate frequencies of acceptance and love, which benefit all beings. Blessing energy rocks in every language.

Love is a great mystery and perhaps Ho'oponopono is simply all about this, love and its rediscovery, about returning to our identity with the Self, back to what is normal and natural, with our Source and all existence. We keep getting hooked back into the data, the story, the bad voodoo, especially whenever we try to assist another; we often get stuck in the data. Most people, who are instructing us on YouTube and the written word, tend to jump right into the mantra for the process and, in my humble opinion, have translated sometimes, the simple wisdom to accommodate patterns and beliefs, what is easy, therefore jumping right back into duality.

Why? There is NO subject in Ho'oponopono. No subject really? We are not launching "pono" at someone. We are only always working on our own balance and harmony. I will say this again. Please, we are only always working on our own balance and harmony. It is an adjustment for me. I have performed over 1,000 ceremonies and been curious about the prayers of all cultures. Now I am just working with the "Self" along with the inquiry, "Who Am I?" and the mantra/prayer/statement, "I Love you, I'm sorry, Please forgive me, Thank you."

Ancient wisdom says, "There is no one to work on out there, only oneself." There is no 'out there' out there. I am using the K.I.S.S method of 'keeping it simple silly' and purposefully not getting creative. I AM trying to find out exactly how Dr. Hew Len does it. This is being revealed to me more as feeling and freedom than any insight. The whole planet is pregnant with fire, electricity, weather changes, and a possible movement to another dimension. Do we try to manage that or surrender to that? When I feel stuck in the mud I leap in faith. Now, I have learned or am learning to leap within. Metaphysical people are reaching out to me in the health club, the bank at the grocery store, unsolicited. I love it. The more I stay inside and work on the mantra/prayer the more doors are opening, and people are resonating.

Dr. Hew Len has a workshop with Joe Vitale on YouTube and I highly recommend it. The purpose of this essay is to simply highlight the points that are very worthy of repetition. The shift from an outer and mental orientation of all healer types needs to be simply, but totally, "turned around and turned within," and this is quite strange at the beginning.

I know this much: Dr. Hew Len does "not" work with intention. He does "not" try to find the negativity inside himself and analyze it. He does not encourage storytelling.

Since doing the Ho'oponopono daily, I would say that I do feel like I have energized a bubble around myself, resulting in a better insulation from the world and its density. I participate more fully it seems. That is a paradox, isolation, and a deeper participation. For myself this has been a very pleasant, new quality to enjoy.

So far as I have found Dr. Hew Len is the only teacher engaging the invocation of the "I AM." I am not saying that some good results may not occur as a result of participating this way without it, with just the four statements. What I AM saying is that the invocations and inner child meditations give the process greater depth and substance, sensitivity, and openness. I am saying that Dr. Hew Len describes the process as Self I-*dentity*. This is a big idea - the "True Self." The concept transcends our small and often self-contracted way of approaching reality. The concept or understanding of "who am I?" is a first concern of a Ho'oponopono enthusiast. That discovery or inquiry is first and foremost. Here begins the concept and contact with the Low Self, the Unihipili in Hawaiian, or the Inner Child, also called the subconscious mind. One must venture to become as a child, turn within, do the breathing, and begin the dialogue with this forgotten aspect of self. You may remember that the saying has been accredited to Jesus that "in order to enter into the kingdom you must be born again."

I would direct you to the "Inner Child meditation" with Dr. Hew Len presentation at https://www.youtube.com/watch?v=gBuZ9sX8wMw&pbjreload=101. With that done, and now having the four statements at your disposal, you are quite prepared to transform your world. Miracles happen! And you are One!

Do the Clearing

Emerge as the Self

Aloha

The source of Ho'oponopono is ancient and comes to us from an oral tradition that is timeless and mysterious. No one knows the origin of Ho'oponopono, just that it is ancient. Somewhat like the Tao of Lao Tsu, who references the sage person as being of the Tao, as being almost unfathomable, somewhat like the wind. The Masters of the Far East have given us the Upanishads, whose authors are unknown to us, and which date back thousands of years before Christ. The "sermon on the mount" is considered an Upanishad and is also referenced as having come to us from ancient Greece, perhaps two hundred years before the birth of Jesus. There are scriptures from India that we know date back five thousand years that give (in one manuscript) one hundred ten different meditation techniques. Rumi and Ibn Arabi (to name just a couple) are most auspicious Sufi poets of the 13th century whose works may never ever be duplicated. The I Ching of China is an oracle and is dated back to 1100 BC. Confucius said upon dying that his only regret in life was that he wished he had discovered the I Ching earlier. Hermetic science dates back a minimum of six thousand years, as examples of tools and technologies found in the articles and books in the pyramids suggest. And then there are the Zen masters. Yes, the ancients had knowledge and wisdom.

Ho'oponopono is, first of all, very sacred. Like the millions of Indians who bathe in the Ganges every year, it might be valuable for us to take a bath, light a candle and a stick of incense, and prepare ourselves when we begin to address the "inner child," and before we petition the inner child or Low Self to speak to our Higher Self on behalf of our Middle Self or person. We must engage the breath in a conscious way. Our habits of being are just that, habits. We might pause a moment or two as we begin to embrace the energies in a prayerful and almost playful way. The focus may be as simple as distinguishing the inner from our outer reality. When you can observe your experience consciously you can venture within to observe adjustments, improvements, and enlightenments. You simply observe. You do not act or make it happen.

Dr. Hew Len opened his workshop with this invocation:

> *I AM the I*
>
> *I come forth from the void into light*
>
> *I AM the breath that nourishes all life*

I AM that Emptiness, that holiness beyond all consciousness

The I, the Id, the All

I draw my bow of rainbows across the waters

The continuum of Mind that matters

I AM the incoming and the outgoing of the breath

The invisible and untouchable breath

I AM the indefinable atom of creation

I AM the I

The Hawaiian concept of the Low, Middle and Higher Self preceded the discoveries of Freud and Jung who ventured to explain the subconscious and collective conscious minds. Many modern talk therapies are proving to be a lot of this, just talk. Time magazine has featured articles on how talking about our history, our story and problems tends not to diminish, but too often, magnify our personal problems and distortions. Mindfulness is the new buzzword, and it is a big word. It turns out that man and mind and nature had a different energetic signature before man and mind and machines, television, cell phones and computers came into everyday use. Some nutrition experts say simply that there are no magic bullets for people on computers over four hours per day. People are spending hours and hours daily with others who have no idea about 100% responsibility of the Ho'oponopono, and in the constant reminder of the problem reality. It is a shame: it is a crime and there are far too many people doing their time. It seems that the whole culture may be in the wrong paradigm.

Blessed are the merciful: for they shall obtain mercy.

Blessed are the pure in heart for they shall see God.

What is 100% responsibility anyway?

It is a shift. It is a simple adjustment to observing in a choice for no data. It is not a guilt trip we put upon ourselves for having created some weird karma or distortion. The shift can only come from you being all in, or 100% responsible. All in is a Yes with a capital Y. When you dive and now you are in the air you are almost in, you are not in yet, but there is no turning back, that's it. That is 100% responsible. You know what I am talking about. That is that. There is no definition for 100% responsibility except it is like diving. When you do dive, your aim is the water. The air is just the proof of commitment.

Sosan, the great Zen teacher, said "the great way is easy for those who have no preferences. Make the smallest distinction however, and heaven and earth are set infinitely apart."

The smallest distinction, only one percent, and we are back in duality, back in the data. Have 100% responsibility to observe the lens being cleared, doing the cleaning, and get back to zero. Is there a learning process? Of course, there is. Please do enjoy this. The best divers prepare by taking off their clothes and shoes, commit and launch.

>I love you = I look upon that water,
>
>I am sorry = I am going to make a splash,
>
>Please Forgive me = what a sound as I hit the surface,
>
>Thank you = I'm in and I'm clean too

The mantra: *"I love you. I am sorry. Please forgive me. Thank you."*

Within the body/mind of the user this produces a back door to escape the negative energy in front of them. You might give yourself, in that moment, a reminder to "seek ye first the kingdom of God and then all things will be added to you." This is referred to as doing the cleaning. This is key. This is a letting go process, but at the same time very energetically positive. It facilitates one in entering into the three-fold process of

#1. Repentance or reconciliation,

#2. Forgiveness, and

#3. Transmutation.

The mantra acts like Mr. Clean on your mental body. Who cares how the dirt got there? Just brush it, just mop it, and just clean it.

Dr. Hew Len, PHD., has demonstrated the miraculous by emptying out a state insane asylum for criminals in Hawaii; he showed that we can observe change by staying out of the data. The data is the garbage that turns in the mind and holds the attention of all those who suffer. That is right. Jump into the Ganges (hypothetically) and out of the data and you will be all right. By the way, Dr. Hew Len did not speak to patients. He simply clears or does the cleaning on what arises in himself when he reflects on someone or something. His contact with his "true" self allows him to reflect and not react and that is very powerful. Return to zero and there are no problems. Data always has noise associated with it. Silence and stillness are the qualities of zero. You said, he said, she said are the data streams playing in the head. Our relationship problems begin with one simple impulse of data, of separation, of programs, of blocks, of distortion. Then we take a history of the mystery and the misery, and around and around in the circle game we go. The clinging, the clutching, the hanging on continues and, if one exits and reenters a place or a person, often after many years, people are not even creative enough to get new and exciting problems. It is just the same old data, often.

Can doing the practice establish an autopilot cleaning service for you? Dr. Hew Len says that when you truly establish the connecting with the Lower Self, the inner child, the subconscious, the Unihipili (Basic Self), that the cleaning becomes automatic. Imagine that! The wisdom of the body that made and maintains the body, regenerates the body and will do this for the mind. But first you must make contact and continue to nurture the relationship.

I like to work with the four statements when I am in the hot tub and sauna at my health club. I do this driving to work, exercising and even when I am doing bodywork. Last week I treated a woman with a frozen shoulder. Her doctor refused to give her more cortisone; her physical therapist sent her for massage. Before her second massage appointment, she was in the reception area demonstrating the full use of her shoulder. I was shocked. I think that her shoulder was full of data, which released. The result was freedom of movement. Stay in a state of grace and let the universe handle the details.

I have done a significant amount of mantra meditation and chanting in my life and Ho'oponopono has an effect like a mantra. Yesterday I received a call from the president of the company I worked for that owes me thousands of dollars in back pay. You might say I got really jerked around by them. I could have gone into the "data," but my observation was that I did not and so I didn't get hooked into the drama. My inner strength is significantly building. I look forward to meditating on the statements and if I have to attend to something in the world, like work, like chopping wood and carrying water, I focus on that and then try to get back into the mantra. *I love you, I'm sorry, Please forgive me, Thank you.*

I do not analyze the statements and just establish a rhythm like mantra meditation; it unwinds the tension in the mind. You might say that (hypothetically) all data has a counterclockwise motion. The mind of the Buddha (you) likes to spin clockwise. The mind likes to have something to do and even this is a great offering to the mind. The result is more peace for sure. Next thing we will be moving mountains. The future is so bright, and we can only get there from here, from presence, balance, and love.

The idea of dialoging with the inner child is a bit strange at first perhaps, but this too becomes a joyful dynamic that is on a higher vibration than our very often-constant self-talk. Self-talk, for most people, is neutral at best. Dr. Hew Len says that this relationship is the most important one of our life. I AM meditating on this idea and I believe I have got some idea why this is. I will leave this open for your discovery.

Data, Memory, or the Bend in the Road

> Simply put, clean the lens and the dirt/data disappears.
> What remains is zero.
> The cost of straightening is only the curve, or distortion.

Many teachings say that what we seem to be upset about is not what we think, but more than likely something that is stimulating a memory of unhealed business. The teachers include Dr. Marrnah Simeona, a Hawaiian Ho'ponopono master teacher as well as being mentioned many times in the *Course in Miracles*, Dr. Hew Len calls it the data. When we experience stress or fear it is associated with an event of the past. This needs clearing, or cleaning. By simply defining this "stuff' as data, we can use this safety net to exit the tendency to "get hooked," to try and control, or even to define and analyze something. Ho'oponopono is a "Don't Analyze This" system. One must begin to trust that "there is nothing in the data." You cannot breathe in and out at the same time. Healing is only about "letting go," loving, forgiving, releasing, and breathing out. We let go and let God. It is a simple enough concept. The execution is a mastery and not ever a misery. The data is always a hook, a story (however exceptional) and a misery. It is not even us who does the forgiveness. You might say that we create a vacuum and allow the divinity to reenter. Do the cleaning and life will do the healing.

> What if every atom in the universe
> Responded to the observer?
> Please be careful how you look there!

100% Responsibility is Liberating

What is going on in me that this problem is showing up?

Problems are not found or discovered in another person. That is their business. All our challenges are found within ourselves. In order to change things, change and transform oneself. Taking total responsibility, 100% responsibility, for one's life means just that, everything in our life, simply because it is in our life: it's our responsibility.

I have found it powerful to consciously speak in the negative to clarify ideas and process. An example of this might be, water is not air. There may be oxygen in water, but water is water. Another example of this might be if you are preparing to leave for work and now you can't find your keys. You drove home last night and used them to open the door. No one visited you.

Your keys did not go out by themselves. They are not lost; you just cannot find them. They are here in YOUR house. Calling them names or getting upset just stores negative energy in the body/mind. Slow down, take a breath, think, and feel and "oh they are right here in my pants pocket." This is how 100% responsibility works. We learn to stop projecting, lose the data, return to balance. When a person is capable of surrendering to the reality of 100% responsibility for everything and anything, then they can grasp inspiration and reduce projection and reaction. Focus within and begin or continue on the path of liberation.

Ho'oponopono is a key for working on oneself and "only on oneself." Later on down the road, we will begin to expand this to other people, places and things, but one will quickly discover that all shifts and breakthroughs and cleaning are the result of the coherence that one has within. Our state of balance matters. Working in the "light" is just that, light. Let go and let the light. This is a unique mindset and approach which will continue to deepen and deepen as we engage the practice and formula. The formula can be interpreted with a subject or without one.

Normally when we say I love you we have another person in mind. We have an 'us' and 'them'. With our us of I love you, we are only speaking to OUR Unihipili, OUR Lower Self, OUR inner child, OUR subconscious mind. It is directed to the data, the memory and emotion arising. There is no other.

We appeal to the data, the material, the emotion, and Divinity does the "cleaning."

I love you, I'm sorry, please forgive me, thank you.

You let go and Divinity does the healing. You let go and Divinity does the erasing. You let go and Divinity does the clearing. You let go and Divinity does the cleaning. We offer the prayer formula to the lower mind, the inner child, which passes this along to the superconscious mind and healing happens. When healing happens, waves and frequency are generated, and this influences our environment and all our relationships. Our inspiration is a seed breath that flowers in its own way, in its own time. Just keep breathing inspiration and cleaning happens.

Other systems move energy around like chess pieces on a board. Ho'oponopono removes the pieces all together. There is no religion attached to the process. There are no gurus. Divinity is the only teacher. You can let go of victim consciousness and embrace victory in awareness. All problems begin as thought and are powered by emotion. 'I love you' said alone releases the past. Some realities, challenges and disappointments are greater opportunities for deeper personal transformation. Practice daily, practice mindfully, and even the biggest problems give way to unique possibilities of transformation, creativity, and light.

Problems are a momentary lapse in knowledge and awareness of how much the creator loves us.

Morrnah Nalamaku Simeona prayer for cleansing goes as follows:

> *Divine Creator, father, mother, and son as one, if I, my family, relatives and ancestors have offended you, your family, relatives and ancestors in thought, word or deed from the beginning of our creation to the present, we ask forgiveness. Let us cleanse, purify, release, cut all negative memories, blocks, energies, vibrations and transmute the unwanted energies to pure light. And it is done.*
>
> Be awed with what God can do! It is not our job to heal people, that is Divinities job.
>
> Do the cleaning
>
> Emerge as the Self
>
> Aloha

Please see Dr. Hew Len's meditation on the Inner Child on YouTube. With that done and now having the four statements at your disposal you are quite prepared to transform your world.

Miracles happen! And you are one.

Thoughts on Hypnotherapy

by Karin Couture

Hypnosis has been utilized by professional healthcare providers, doctors, and psychologists for many hundreds of years. There are many ways we can use hypnosis or hypnotherapy to enhance our lives. We use hypnotherapy to change behaviors that do not serve us well in living our lives to our fullest potential.

Hypnotherapy can be helpful to persons of all ages. The benefits of hypnotherapy are many, broad and deep. Simply put, hypnosis is a tool for relaxation: relaxation of the mind, and for strengthening the relationship of the subconscious, conscious and some might even say, your superconscious mind. Stop smoking or weight loss hypnosis programs can be very effective in making the desired changes for these behaviors, and there are also many others that we can change.

Hypnotherapy can assist us to alter habits, behaviors, and release traumas that affect us negatively, because hypnotherapy gets to the root of the issue. It does not have to take years to make positive changes when you can focus your inner healer on any issue and begin to make positive changes, often very immediately and directly. Depending on the issue, a behavior oftentimes can be changed in one or two sessions.

We may not consciously understand exactly why we behave in a certain way or react the way we do in a circumstance such as public speaking or having nervousness before taking a test, just to name a couple. Hypnotherapy allows us to uncover something that is preventing us from doing these tasks without fear. You can tell yourself you can do something or think you can do something, but often when it's time to do this action, something prevents you from being able to perform the task at hand. This is because there is something in the mind that is blocking us. Going in and recording new possibility patterns gives us more open and direct options on how to perform desired actions in our lives. This is key to any mental process.

Hypnotherapy is the way to access the subconscious mind to make changes in our behavior so we can live our lives freely without the baggage, patterns and behaviors that hold us back. By going deep into relaxation, we bypass the conscious or logical mind to establish healthy probability patterns. It is not necessary to discover the causes of prior limitations, it is sufficient to just relax and re-inform yourself.

Hypnotherapy is totally safe and ethical. At no time will you be given any instructions that run contrary to your morals and ethics.

Hypnotherapists can create scripts that are custom, tailor made specifically for the client. When I work over the phone with a client, I record the session and then email to the client for their use at home. Scripts are empowering and can be used in the privacy of one's own home at a time when it is most convenient.

Hypnotherapy is such a marvelous tool to utilize to enhance our lives and to become fearless in living. There are many areas that can be alleviated and corrected through the use of hypnotherapy. Here is a list of a few of them:

Fingernail biting	Anorexia (eating disorders)
Bed wetting	Confidence
Stuttering	Enhancing memory
Illnesses	Dyslexia
Insomnia	Phobias
Dental work	Improving Sports abilities
Depression	High Blood Pressure
Anxiety	Incontinence
Stress Management	Money matters
Trauma	Motivation
PTSD	Self Esteem

The list goes on and on.

Hypnotherapy is such a useful tool; it can encompass all areas of life. If there is something holding you back or creating discomfort in your life, hypnotherapy is an easy and painless way to get on with the business of living in a more comfortable and stress-free manner.

Please contact me if you would like to explore creating a made to order script to move onward and upward on your journey. Requests/questions can be sent to: Attn: Karin http://lifeseedcodes.com

Get started now. Complimentary script available upon request.

Why I Don't Tell People What to do, What to Think or What to Believe

Four Reasons: The 4 Agreements, 4 Ho'oponopono, 4 Immeasurables

The Four Agreements of the Toltec Wisdom are:

Be Impeccable in your word.
Don't take anything personal.
Don't make assumptions.
Always do your best.

The Ho'oponopono statements are:

I Love you, I'm sorry, please forgive me, thank you.

The Four Immeasurables

Unconditional Loving,
Compassion,
Sympathetic Joy,
and Equanimity

What are the Four Immeasurables (The Four Sublime States)?

The Four Immeasurables, also known as The Four Sublime States, were a subject very dear to the heart of the Buddha. He spoke of them often. A person can achieve rebirth in a Brahma realm through the practice and attainment of the Four Sublime States: unconditional love, compassion, sympathetic joy, and equanimity.

Yes, I love wisdom in any and all forms. I told my friend in a statement I had never said or heard before, "if you take the four agreements seriously, you will meet the Buddha on the road, period". You can get from Toltec to the Buddha to the Kahuna without crossing your mind.

Our children have a natural spiritual instinct in many cases and are mindful because we treated them mindfully and lovingly. They are truthful. They strive to do their best. They do not take things personally. They move forward without dwelling in the past. They inspire me! And truthfully, I do not know whether they make assumptions or not. My oldest daughter told me she noticed a copy of the *Four Agreements* by Don Miguel Ruiz, a book about Toltec wisdom, on her boyfriend's coffee table. That affirmed she was in the right place. She does mindfulness meditation. Her Buddhism bonded with his Toltec and they have a beautiful connection. Our children are being guided from within. They do not need a religion shoved down their throats. They get it and are doing what they need to do to fulfill their covenants with life. They have spiritual practices they are on top of. Below I list some disciplines and why I practice the religion of "not telling people what to do, what to think, or what to believe."

Reason #1: 40 years ago, I studied Hakomi work with Ron Kurtz. Hakomi is an organic body-centered psychotherapy process. These practitioners never ever give advice. They do not jump in or on clients. Instead they guide people within to direct experience. They use mindfulness and compassion.

I trained with Ron for a few years and it really was not for many years later that I appreciated just how magical it is. I lived in Boulder one summer at Ron's house. About 35 years later they celebrated a global Hakomi day. Thank you Lord Buddha; thank you Lao Tsu; thank you Ron. We are learning slowly to be more mindful, quiet, and compassionate. We are learning to stay out of people's business.

Reason #2: In Alphabiotics we do energy balancing and brain hemisphere integration. We do not tell people what to do, think or believe. We simply reset the biocomputer and let the wisdom of the body heal the body. It is very liberating to *not* have to have people's answers. Once I worked with a man who stuttered for 14 years. We worked together to balance his energy for 14 months and he stopped stuttering. What the heck do I know? His wisdom of the body healed his body!

Reason #3: In neurotherapy training in Self-Hypnosis I trained, got certified and received 75 sessions. We never asked the subconscious questions. We did not make suggestions. We did not play God. Our plan was to help a person reach alpha and theta states and develop the ability to do this for themselves by practicing daily. It works! Many people who had serious mental/emotional complications that were not able to get relief from other systems and professionals had major breakthroughs. We did not give advice. We did not rush in where angels feared to tread. We did not tell people what to do, what to think, and what to believe.

Reason #4: The Diamond Heart Energy Activations are downloads of "light" that assist people in raising their vibration levels. We muscle test people before we facilitate our sessions to get an idea of their integration levels. To this point, the highest level of integration of the body-mind-spirit, or actually of the body elemental-outer personality (personal self) and the guardian angel, has been 65%. The range for the average person is 40% to 65%. The activation has proven to raise peoples' percentages considerably. If you want to raise your vibration and keep it high "you have to do the work" of clearing out ancestral energy, karma, patterns, habits and programs, and engrams. One might evoke the light every day of one's life because there is a lot of bad collective energy we are exposed to. Also, when we sleep, we leave the body and pass through the astral plane and enter back through it. The astral plane is full of garbage, including shadow and disembodied spirits stuck in their desire bodies. People do not benefit at all by having any hitchhikers attached to their energy. A simple universal invocation done daily does wonders. Here is one I use frequently.

The Great Invocation

From the point of light within the mind of God let light pour forth into the minds of men. Let light descend on Earth.

From the point of love within the heart of God may love pour forth into the hearts of men. May the Christ consciousness prevail.

From the center where the will of God is known let purpose quide the little wills of men, the purpose that the masters know and serve.

From the center, which we call the race of man, may the plan of love and light work out and may it seal off the place where evil dwells.

Let love and light and power restore the plan on earth.

Freedom, respect, equanimity, and human dignity are paramount in the Diamond Heart work. I will include our intake form at the end of this essay explaining "What the D.H.E.A. Is Not." One thing we avoid is telling people what to do, what to think, and what to believe.

Good work in healing can happen when we invoke the quantum field or unconscious, the Higher Self, or presence. Facilitators can embrace the Tao without having to be all things to all people. To me it is a sign of maturity to see facilitators practice mindfulness and trust. The 11th commandment is "Don't sweat the small stuff." By not sweating the small stuff people are supported by a wholesome understanding that wisdom is within us and accessible by doing the work and trusting mindfulness and compassion. *All people have equal access to the light within.* The universe does not play favorites. Everybody needs to do the work!

Trust the seasons, trust the Four Reasons, trust the Four Agreements, trust in mindfulness and trust your silence. Oh, and don't forget the 11th commandment and "do not sweat the small stuff."

Yesterday I was doing a bodywork session on another massage therapist who asked me for a reading, right then and there. I did some dowsing and clearing work with her but, I was quick to point out, I do not tell people what to do, what to think, or what to believe. It is not so simple as it sounds, and one will occasionally slip up. The best thing to do when we think we have a remedy or resolution is to stop and make a detour right back to principle.

Healing happens when the quantum field and energy are invited into our minds and bodies. Healing happens when the wisdom of the body is aligned and balanced, and when our spirit is loved, acknowledged, and appreciated. I AM the Resurrection of my Body, Mind and Spirit.

Seven Stages of Consciousness

The following article is used by permission by John Kanary

The mind is an unlimited resource. We have seen such incredible growth in recent decades to prove it: exponential growth in industry, technology, agriculture, spirituality, and an awareness of humanity in general. This growth, this accelerated evolution of the human experience, is a direct result of our consciousness striving from creation to exhilaration. The limitless expanse of potential in our mind dwarfs the puny physical realm. The mind truly is an unlimited resource.

Tapping into this resource begins by first understanding how it works, understanding the nature of consciousness to the best of our research and ability. Of course, these definitions and correlations are constantly evolving with new discoveries, new insights, and social evolutions. We can begin with certain elastic notions of our experience, which can be outlined succinctly and accessibly in the following way.

Consciousness can be assigned to awareness but is not limited to the notion of relation or relativity. It is not just the relation to events, but also includes the processing of those events, the development of paradigms in the mind, habits in the social sphere and physiological executions of each. Consciousness encompasses so much more than awareness. It is not an exclusive aspect of the human experience as it has yet to have clearly defined and agreed upon boundaries. For this article, we will assign consciousness to our awareness of self and the outside world, the processing of that information and our chosen response to that information.

In this model there are 7 Stages of Consciousness:

Level 1 – Animal

"The drive to survive"

At this level, the focus is on basic security, food, water, shelter and any other basic needs to maintain survival. This is a very self-centered and undeveloped consciousness. Abraham Maslow referred to these as "deficiency" needs. We feel no sense of lasting satisfaction from being able to meet these needs, but we feel a sense of anxiety if these needs are not met. It is a cyclical state of being.

We master Level 1 by developing the practical skills that are necessary to ensure our physical survival.

Level 2 – Mass Consciousness

"The drive for pleasure and the perpetuation of the species."

This level is the social, relationship-based level of consciousness; the desire to be loved, to belong and the awareness of the needs of others. This is above the self-interested level of satisfying physiological needs where we desire emotional fulfillment through communion with others.

We master Level 2 by developing the interpersonal relationship skills that are necessary to feel safe and to be loved.

Level 3 – Aspiration

"The drive for conquest, achievement, victory and esteem."

This is our positive self-esteem, a sense of pride in who we are in the social sphere. Our personal self-worth in relation to our outside world is of intrinsic value, defining ourselves in relation to others and recalibrating those definitions in relation to choices and actions.

We master Level 3 by developing the emotional skills that are necessary to feel good about ourselves in all situations - developing our self-respect.

Level 4 – Individual

"The drive for community or union."

This is a truly transformational state as we rise above the self-interested level of satisfying needs. We begin our journey in learning to master the power of the subconscious mind, identifying paradigms and limiting beliefs and deciding what is acceptable and what is not, and travel a path of self-actualization. We develop a system of values by which we will live our lives and an understanding of our potential impact within our community, in history and our world.

We master Level 4 by learning to release the subconscious and conscious fears we hold concerning the first three levels of needs and thereby begin the process of blending the needs of the ego with the needs of the soul.

Level 5 - Discipline

"The drive for creative self-expression"

Clarity of purpose is aligning your life with your passion and purpose, discovering your authentic self, and making commitments to fulfill those directives that will bring meaning to your life. This is the galvanization and cohesion of our preferred self. We choose to align our Middle Self with our Higher Self by creating a vision for our future and acting in accordance with that vision, action with a definite non-negotiable plan to manifest the universe expressing creation through us.

We master Level 5 when we discover our personal transcendent meaning for existence, our clarity of purpose.

Level 6 - Experience

"The drive to imagine what could be but has yet to be."

Our consciousness has evolved to a point where we recognize that actualization of our sense of purpose, to truly make a difference, is dependent on mutual benefit and fulfillment with others and the collective imagination and development of that which is yet to be.

We master Level 6 by actualizing our sense of meaning by making a difference in the world.

Level 7 - Mastery

"The drive to grasp and take hold of what has been imagined at level 6."

This transcendent state of awareness is self-explanatory.

We master Level 7 when making a difference becomes a way of life, and we embrace the concept of self-less service.

Throughout history and across the world there are cultures that have explored the definitions of these levels of consciousness. Culturally, they may be referred to as cycles, chakras, metals of alchemy, planets of astrology or a myriad of other possible things. The human experience over the centuries has proven that, while there are variations on a theme, and while the potential is limitless, the progress of our consciousness *can* be gauged if not only as a point of reference for evolving and progressing to another level.

We hope that by providing this information, this gauge, you are excited and inspired to explore ways and means of tapping into your unlimited resource to move yourself forward into a new state of consciousness and awareness, thereby accelerating your results, unlocking mysteries within yourself and discovering your authentic self and what you are truly capable of achieving in this precious life.

Thank you to Mr. John Kanary for permission to include these insights and research in my book. You can find more from his website at http://www.johnkanary.com/7-stages-of-consciousness/.

PART THREE

SPIRIT

CHAPTER 7

Introduction to the Spirit

This third section is for the brave of heart.

I AM delighted that I can offer this *FREE* access to the Diamond heart Energy activations. Use the Drop Box instructions to download the meditations.

I AM PRESENCE WORKBOOK

I recently spoke with a woman in New York State who had before and after aura photography done after about ten weeks of daily meditations using the activations and she was most happy with the changes to her energy field. She was holding much more light than before. This was clear to her.

Our alignment with our "I AM" Presence is truly the best way to approach our lives. Life is better in balance. Being open to being guided by our Higher Self is key. These essays will bring a little more light into your life. In essence it is all and always about the "light." We will be unfolding in it forever. Each one of us advances upon the journey of Self-awareness at our own speed and according to our own dispositions. Enjoy the work and feel free to contact me with any questions and of course with any discoveries. We are all in this together.

The alignment of the Body-Mind-Spirit is the discipline of eternity. Be ye therefore as disciplined as possible. Here are more codes for your success and enjoyment. And always remember to 'share freely.' Do the Diamond Heart Energy Activations with friends and family. The activations can be done in massage and bodywork sessions for a deeper journey into "light."

Enjoy.

CHAPTER 8

ESSAYS ON SPIRIT

On Wisdom and Inspiration

We no longer allow an ideal to be forced upon us. We are convinced that in each of us, if only we probe deep enough into the very heart of our beings, there dwells something noble, something worthy of development. We no longer believe that there is a norm of human life to which we all must strive to conform. We regard the perfection of the whole as depending on the unique perfection of each single individual. We do not want to do what anyone else can do equally well.

> *No, our contribution to the development of the world, however trifling, must be something, which by reason of the uniqueness of our nature, we alone can offer. Never have artists been less concerned about the rules and norms in art than today. Each of them asserts his or her right to express in creations of his or her art what is unique to them.*
>
> The Philosophy of Freedom, Rudolf Steiner 1916
> Translation RF Alfred Hoernle

Last, but not least, the important thing is to not stop questioning. Curiosity has its own reason for existing. One cannot help but be in awe when one contemplates the mystery of eternity, of life, of the miraculous structure of reality. It is enough if one tries to merely comprehend a little of the mystery every day. Never lose a holy curiosity.

Albert Einstein, 1879-1955

Our Evolution

Our evolution is a result of the interplay of our habits of being, of our focus and of our creativity. Good habits generate good outcomes. Our focus finds our spirits manifesting through the lens of mind and body. Creativity is our I AM signature on our life and the world around us. Creativity is sometimes synonymous with mystery because, through this, we give birth to new ideas and these ideas take form and shape new possibilities for ourselves. This affects our past, present, and future.

Some say we create our own reality. I am not sure I believe this to be true. One might be safe to assume that we are co-creating our own reality. This demands awareness of Source, symmetry, energy, frequency, and may indeed prove to be our principal purpose in life, to grow creating, co-creating.

On Meditation

One can have a mind made sense of self or a self-made mind of awareness. This takes time, discipline, methods, systems, teachers, commitment, and awareness. Wisdom is attached to those who grow from experience. The logs that cross the roads we travel on hide from view the gift that awaits our safe crossing. In other words, there is plenty of contrast to go around. Most of the time the logs just represent the headaches we produce from complaining too much about the inconveniences. We spend too much energy in complaint mode. Meditation is empty of all this noise. Compassion is the natural state of those who are empty of data, distortion. Once we drop all the non-essentials we are left with a different reality, which is best discovered in silence.

If meditation were the practice of any focused awareness, then consciousness is the awareness of this/that awareness. In the West we have psychologists and the problem reality. In the East we have teachers of movement arts, martial arts, yoga, and meditation. The solution reality embraces the need for growth, for spiritual unfolding. I did a one-day training with a Tibetan Lama who gave us a powerful meditation technique that had historically been only given to the monks. Why was that? The Wisdom Ones see the complexity of the times and the need for clarity. In essence, the workshop was about one thing, *looking*. Or I might say it was about looking and seeing.

Our Lama said, "we teach you how to look and what you see is up to you." The study of Buddhism reveals that it is not a religion, but a psychological system to help us unravel the stuff of ancestral energies, karma, cultural complexities and personal confusion in the hopes and expectations of unfolding our true nature, our Buddha nature. Also, now that we have moved into the quantum age, we have terms like "the vortex" to define the "kingdom within." When I began exploring yoga many years ago and wanted to learn to meditate there was a lot of attention on religious systems and the personalities attached to them. Today we can move into and explore mindfulness practice or technology like Brain Entrainment or guided meditations on YouTube.

Awareness of the "Self" or your "Vortex" happens in the present moment, in the now, and is discovered layer by layer as a result of grace, guidance, practice and maturity. The distractions of our youth give way to greater sense and appreciation of essence, of space and continuity, and mindfulness.

The *Book of Secrets* reveals 110 different meditation techniques that come from texts over three thousand years ago from India, of course. There is a technique for everyone. We also have great help from the Brain Entrainment or Hemi-Sync systems, which can assist us in achieving a greater sense of well-being. A company named Sacred Acoustics has many entry level and advanced levels of sound wave Alpha, Theta, and Delta programs that are powerful modalities. I find myself moving fluidly from mindfulness practice and mantras to headphones and beautiful brain entrainment CD's. I swim with a waterproof MP3 player and listen to a variety of sound wave enhancements.

Although I am initiated in many methods, am a certified hypnotherapist and Bija meditation initiate, I highly recommend the Sacred Acoustics programs for adults and children. I have purchased a complete set of the CD's for myself, my kids and my grandchildren. We are all on the program and are all evolving together. Any type of turning within will always result in greater balance and harmony. They say you never know just what you might find, peace, power, joy, health, and prosperity. It is all there for the having if we are willing to do the practice, and the work.

There is the free 12 minute I AM Meditation at LifeSeedCodes.com that has a unique cleansing effect by invoking the light and grounding into the energies of Mother Earth. At the completion of the guided meditation is the Bija Seed mantra "Hrim" which is a vibration and pulse, which can take one into a deep state of relaxation and awareness.

Diamond Heart Energy Activations

Connecting with one's own "I AM Presence" is the goal and intention of the Diamond Heart Energy Activations. Some say we are moving into the 'I AM Age" where the focus of individual development and well-being is being balanced by the directing of our attention inward and towards the Self. We are doing this through a variety of meditation, self-awareness, and body mindfulness practices. This is the underlying theme of all the work in the Diamond Heart: to become better balanced, and to be creative with greater and greater self-awareness. The relationship of you to <u>you</u> is central. Becoming more of a being that is inwardly guided is the key. The five steps in the guided programs represent first, the explanation of each download; second, the 12-minute guided meditation and visualizations; third, the invocations; fourth, healing mantras; and step five, the closing. This takes about 55 minutes.

Each participant makes a request out loud from their own Higher Self. Like all good things the energy flows from above downwards and from inside out. Our alignment with our physical body, our surface self or personality and our higher mind is the purpose of the first activation. One can call this a body-mind-spirit attunement. One can also acknowledge our body intelligence or body elemental in this process. One can bring the subconscious mind, conscious mind, and the higher mind into harmony. Our superconscious mind has many names such as our guardian angel or our Christ conscious mind in the western culture, our Buddha nature in some cultures, or Atman in yet another. We prefer to call this an "I AM" process and alignment. When our physical/outer self makes deeper contact with our own "spirit," it is quite universal in nature and definition. One's individual power is simply awaiting the call. Proper focus and intention are ways of awakening latent energy within.

Initially the activations were done as meditations and only after they were recorded did the layering of energy through hands-on healing work come into play. In other words, by keeping a person turned within and layering light, energy and healing we really seemed to become even more effective. We offer and teach the Alpha Brain Body Balancing, but we affirm that all conscious hands-on processes will be effective when sharing the process with others, friends, or family.

With most people the level of integration of body, mind and spirit is between 50% to 65%. We muscle test people to determine this degree or percentage. In practice, we are able to shapeshift and facilitate an alignment for most people and bring them to

90% or 100% integration. This feels amazing! Although it is not always possible to resonate at this level at all times, the 12 minute I AM Presence Meditation, which is offered as a free download on the LifeSeedCodes.com web site, will assist you to maintain the high level, as will any practice of your choosing. If we pick up discordant energies, run negative programs and/or become unbalanced in our Chakras, which is inevitable as we move about our lives, our rate of vibration suffers, and our level of integration diminishes. Invoking the "light" daily is a positive action to keep in-tune with the "I AM Presence" and raise our vibration. Everyone is welcome to use, in any capacity personally or professionally, the 12 steps or guided meditations available at Amazon books: *I Am Presence: Diamond Heart Energy Activation Workbook* by Brian Roberts, published June 20, 2016.

Training in Alpha Brain Body balancing is available. Get to know thyself better by going on an inward journey of discovery. Get tapped in, tuned in, turned on and embrace your Diamond Heart and your very own I AM Presence. I AM the resurrection and the life of my body, mind, and spirit.

Original music on all 12 guided meditations by the author, Brian Roberts

Art design and concepts and Wave Reiki by Karin Couture

Access to the 12 Guided Activation/Meditations

I am delighted that you have arrived here to begin a fabulous journey with the Diamond Heart Energy Activations.

Work with one activation per week only. Do this as often as you like.

Or as a minimum do the activation once and support this by daily use of track # 2, the 12 minute I AM Meditation.

Create a separate play list for the I AM Meditation (track # 2) so that you can listen and then relax afterwards in the energy of the mantra.

The Heart Mantra at the end of this meditation is sufficient for advanced meditators. Eventually you can do a meditation on this mantra alone. However, the complete guided meditation, with visualizations and focus on the breath, is a fantastic way to practice aura and energy maintenance and develop an inward way.

It is best to create a folder and individual playlists for each of the activations in iTunes and download all the materials, as the password will be changing each week.

Please honor that you have paid for the program and let others who might participate order and pay for the workbook, *I Am Presence: Diamond Heart Energy Activation Workbook* by Brian Roberts, to receive the activations.

Share them in your practice; then let people purchase them at Amazon through the workbook.

Contact me for a complimentary remote energy clearing / or LifeWeaving session at 206 799 5605 or email me at Lifeseed108@hotmail.com

We are here to support you in every way we can. Blessings from Brian & Karin

Welcome to Drop Box
Access to Activations here:

https://www.dropbox.com/sh/0agguy77h4zb5pz/AAAvPdf2U1Bx7QcWf-saOOVfVa?dl=0

Download Directions

1. Open iTunes (its free) and click on "New Playlist."
2. Choose "Activation," then click on again and play.
3. A box will then appear that says "Download." Click there. (On my IMac the activations go to the download folder.)
4. Now open the "New Playlist" window on iTunes.
5. Click on "New" and slide right to "Play List."
6. Now drag the tracts into the playlist. Be sure to do a separate playlist for each activation.

Now you are ready to go

My website is http://LifeSeedCodes.com.

Praise Your Diamond Self

by Edna Ballard

All great, illumined minds agree that the God-Self in each of us is free, all-powerful, all-knowing, and everywhere present; that It is our life in all Its good, true, and harmonious impulses and is therefore *perfection*.

One would think that when we give this subject our attention, we would all realize as a self-evident fact that it is the most important part of us and, therefore, should receive the major portion of our time, energy, and effort. Yet, many there are who never devote any particular thought, time or attention to the only source from which our happiness comes. Too often we fail to think of our Source or inquire into the laws governing our lives and affairs until some problem, more than ordinarily troublesome, demands solution.

The greatest things in the universe are done in absolute silence. Nature, when she accomplishes her greatest marvels, works in silence.

The Diamond Self has been referred to as "The Voice of the Silence." It sounds like a paradox perhaps, yet it is absolutely true. If each of us would take a few moments several times a day, sit quietly and listen to the silence inside of our own bodies, we would receive much rest and illumination with very little effort.

If, during our moments of inward contemplation, we thank, praise, and bless our Diamond Self for the many good things we are receiving every moment, or if we just give praise for the good there is in each experience as we pass through it, we would be astonished at the increase in the blessings we attract into our lives. The Bible says that: " ... the scepter shall not depart from Judah," and the word Judah here means "praise."

Praise keeps the human self in an attitude of expansion, for it is a giving out, which opens the way for the Diamond Self to pour forth the gifts of the kingdom. Love, praise, and blessings are the tao, or pathway, over which the Diamond Self sends its glories into manifestation. It is the magnet which sends down into the individualized consciousness, the Perfection of the Absolute. Service, when lovingly given, is also a magnet to make heaven manifest on earth. As the Diamond Self has manifested a form for each of us, through which to pour out Its perfection, let us every day give It at least as much time and attention as we do to the eating of our meals.

If we decide to get an education along any particular line in the physical world, or the without, let us try to give at least a third as much time to educating and attuning our human self to the receiving of instruction and illumination from the within. This is most easily accomplished through love, praise, and the expression of gratitude to the Diamond Self. A little continued practice will convince the most skeptical of the practical side of this effort. The lawyer spends many years, giving all his time every day, to the study of what we call human law. The psychologist gives much the same amount of time and energy to the study of trying to understand the laws under which the human mind operates. In school, we are taught the laws of this, that, and the other physical operation.

Let us consider what the same amount of time and energy devoted to getting acquainted with our Diamond Self will do for us. One hour each day, say thirty minutes in the morning and thirty minutes in the evening, in love, adoration, praise and communion with our Diamond Self - asking It to tell us about Itself and to illumine all things for us as we contact them each day - will bring us more permanent growth, happiness and accomplishment than any physical study we can indulge in.

Let us definitely get acquainted with our Diamond Self, which after all is the powerhouse of the universe. The quickest way is through praise, love, and gratitude; and for even the little that we give, we receive infinitely in return. There is no such thing as failure to the Diamond Self,

To those who comrade with the King of Kings, there is no opposition. Let us go to school once more, become as little children and be taught by Him who knows all. There will be nothing we cannot do when we have learned that He is the only Doer.

If we will dare to turn away from our sense consciousness and listen to the Voice that speaks in the silence within us, we will be living at the heart of our being. There we shall be shown and taught what never in all eternity can be learned in the world without. The Diamond Self, knowing all and having all under control, can flash to us in an instant an entire lifetime of experience. This does not mean that we should leave the outer mind unperfected by education and cultivation of the intellect. The human mind must be taught order, system and focus of the energies to a single point. It does mean, however, that we should give at least as much time and attention to that which is permanent as to that which changes.

The Diamond Self is the only source of permanent happiness. We are all seeking that and, he who will, may enter in and be taught by the Knower of all knowledge. Praise, love, and gratitude for the good which exists in everything, will move mountains. It is the royal road to peace, happiness, and perfection.

If we give all our time, attention and energy to the little selfish self and its human desires, we have no right to expect the good things of life to be given us by the Diamond Self. Until we are willing to give this Larger Self our all, and put It first, we need never expect and have no right to ask for our freedom and happiness. Therefore, there is only one real law of life and that is: Be loyal to your Diamond Self. Praise it! Bless it! Worship it! Adore it! Put it first above all else and it will open the flood gates and pour out treasures beyond your fondest dreams. Loyalty to it is all it demands of you and me, and that is no more than an ordinary businessman asks of the employees to whom he pays his money. Surely, we can be as fair in our attitude to this beautiful giver of every good and perfect gift as we are to the business world.

Therefore, praise, praise, and praise your Diamond Self during every waking moment. Experience what it means to be a child of the emperor of the universe here and now, physically, mentally, and spiritually. So shall the Kingdom of Heaven be made manifest on Earth, under grace, in His name and service.

Shaman's Creed/ Quantum Self/ Healer Oath

Begin each day anew on the school and testing ground of Earth, walking in balance, upright, avoiding the chaos of the world. Be "in" the world but "not of it." It is yours to know, to dare, to dream, to will and to remain within, to remain in one's power, to be silent. Only bring no harm of thought, in word, or deed, see to the transmutation of shadow into light. Observe the cyclical nature of things.

Speak the truth of being, never boasting, never proud; just a smooth and refined presence, supported from within, and leading with the heart, is necessary. Inspire when possible. Educate through focused action and example. In this freedom you release the desire to see other people change. This release brings one closer to one's power. Embrace this fluidity. While a man may falter, the universe never fails, never falters on its path.

Step aside duality and observe the unity of things, oneness and fluidity can be enjoyed even amongst the loud and the crowd. A younger soul might wobble or slide aside a slippery road. Turn within and remember the true north. It is time for the phoenix to rise. Now is the ascension of the light. Travel light, no baggage here to carry of journey's past. Empty! And arise! Now! Be the resurrection of the body, mind, and spirit. Be as you are!

Integration and synergistic waves of frequency, awareness, and color map out new vistas of possibility. You can listen and learn and hear the universe humming when returning to the breath, to the self, to what's true and light. Renew oneself often in breath and being.

That which has a front has a back. There are shadows out there where there are phantoms of mind and smoke, and the sun does not shine. Listen, pass the frozen zones where devoid of spirit lay empty, waiting their turn. There is just the wrong combination of elements that will release, reshape, re-gather in time.

Be aware and be able to unfold what does lay inside you for the benefit of life, regardless of how seemingly small or majestic. It is all a play, a dance of particles of light, space and time always returning, always re-birthing. The sage is fueled by the sun, and the sorcerer is tuned to "Source," where all that is required is made present, light, but bountiful. Your channel opens and now is just the energy flow, it is natural, and it cycles from here to there and yet remains, like the river moving to the sea, always moving, always present. ʟ

Just as wisdom cannot be forced upon us, it comes from experience, a virtue, a patience, an appreciation, embodied within a wholesome smile, a lightness of touch, a hesitation that acknowledges wonder in its own timing, place, and of its own origin. All wonder flows from the "One." I need not take anything too personal on this road of life and death and life. First a rock, then a plant, then an animal, then a man/woman, then a _____. This is the way the universe flows through us. Remain open!

Nurturing love universally brings us through those challenging times of doubt or despair. When a focused discipline is cloaked in softness and subtlety, movements through halls and up the stairs of life are guaranteed to bring us to the tables of desire and creativity, fulfilled and not wanting. Each new step is a master plan now unfolding when I AM being.

I think therefore I AM. I love therefore I BE, belonging in this sea of life.

Inspired by the *Desiderata* of Max Ehrmann

A Quantum Self/ A Shaman' Creed by Brian T Roberts.

The Philosophy and Processes Go Like This:

Hakomi

These are the Freedom Attitudes:
- Mindfulness, Non-Violence
- Self-Reflective, Self-Organizing
- Self-Healing, Presence
- Non-Ordinary States of Consciousness not Data
- Non-Force and Holistic
- Assisted Self Inquiry
- Compassion and Trust

Diamond Heart Energy Activations
What the Activations are Not

These are the Principals:
- Not a form of therapy
- Not a religious belief system
- Not diagnostic
- Not a belief system
- Participants are free to stop, it's all voluntary
- No suggestions
- No advice
- No recruiting
- No hierarchy
- No karma

Alphabiotics

Innate wisdom is more intelligent than any practitioner.
We do not tell people what to do, or what to think, or what to believe.
Only the wisdom of the body can heal the body

Neuro-Therapy
Training in Self Hypnosis

When training in self-hypnosis we are not injecting our ideas or extracting materials from the subconscious mind. Trainers trust the inner power of the mind at rest and in harmony. We teach you how to look. Discovery is personal.

There is never a footprint left behind.

Bija Meditation Initiation

Mantras transcend religious beliefs and attitudes and direct the participant inward toward the Self.

Each personal session in working with a Bija mantra is the equivalent of seeing a healer for a session. That's powerful.

Statement of Clarity

What is consistent is the honoring of the person, their innate intelligence and the Presence, Field, or the Unconscious mind. Letting go and letting flow is the central theme of all healing or returning to wholeness.

These are the principles I work with as mindfully as I can in the moment. When I practice with people I try and experience people as the gods that they are. The past is history. The present, or presence is the magic and the mystery. Believe and receive, doubt and do without.

In other words, there is a time and place for therapy, and we wish those who choose to do some, great success.

However, reorganizing oneself on to a higher level of self-awareness and improved function is more like wellness work and the simple magic of healing, a return to a natural state.

Collaboration is a real thing of beauty.

Healing is a spiritual thing in action.

Ascension

Gnosticism, the Mind of the Buddha, the Living Christ, and the Diamond Heart

Gnosticism is the teaching based on Gnosis, the knowledge of transcendence arrived at by way of internal, intuitive means. Religions of all variety are based in belief. There are both belief systems and developmental systems, which sometimes overlap. The Buddha never spoke of God, and the Dali Lama said that studying Buddhism would make one a better Christian because, like Gnosticism, Buddhism is most definitely a way of self-awareness and purification. The Ten Commandments tell us what not to do, while the Noble Eightfold Path defines an approach to purification resulting in the end of suffering through the cultivation of wisdom, ethical conduct, and a mental discipline which will potentially result in enlightenment.

Prayer and meditation are very different. Although many, while as a part of meditation practice, may use prayer in their spiritual practice, meditation is an art that requires a very definite commitment to training the mind and body. Lots of people have religious beliefs and are even willing to fight about them. The mind of the Buddha or Christ has no fight or resistance left in it.

Like Buddhism, Gnosticism begins with the fundamental recognition that earthly life is filled with suffering. Christianity is practiced by many to get to heaven. There are far too many other ideas about it to mention or even to speculate upon. Most people wash with water, some with soap and water. Water has a different name in every culture but is essentially the same all over the world. I once trained with a Buddhist Lama who always said, "We can teach you how to look, what you find is up to you."

The Diamond Heart Energy Activations are celebrations of our inner connections to One's I AM Presence within. The practice of guided meditations; with the use of music, visualizations, invocations, mantras, affirmations and breathing awareness, deliver us to alpha and theta states. By quieting the outer mind, we become more intimate with the inner creative mind and aspects of one's own true spiritual anatomy. Imagine what the caterpillar realized when it became the butterfly.

Use of imagination and creativity are required to get what you want. Meditation is a way to discover what you want. When we have one-pointedness of mind, we are aware that we also have a Buddha nature, that Christ Consciousness is a goal, direction, and accomplishment within. We cannot be limited by belief, but instead move beyond belief into higher and higher states of unfolding consciousness that have no ends or limitations; we keep ascending.

Although meditating in a cave may be optimal, it is certainly not practical. One does not drive one's car in a theta state. The world is pretty much functioning in beta, sometimes rough and loud. Healing happens in alpha states. Transcendence happens in a theta state. Deep contact with spirit may require developing an ability to stay in a delta state with awareness. One can practice the "I AM Presence" meditation daily. One can use the 12 Diamond Heart Energy Meditations on a weekly basis, over and over again.

When we offer the celebration of the Diamond Heart Energy Activations, we are working in ascension in a very practical way. Any time we "raise our vibration" we are ascending. By attuning ourselves with our SELF, we empower ourselves to navigate the life that is already God-given. We can respond with love and react less in fear when we have access to the light within ourselves. The journey of a thousand miles begins with one single step, then another, then another.

Our celebrations include bodywork and Alpha Brain Body Balancing. This is a very gentle, but powerful, fight or flight mechanism release, which results in brain hemisphere synchronization. We invite all participants to join in after giving simple instructions. We are equal opportunity activators. Everyone can have the activations, and anyone can learn to do them and extend the love, light, and energy to others. Because unity is the goal in God, blessing one another is one way of living, loving, and learning. The Diamond Heart Energy Activations are intended to be just that, a blessing mechanism. One heart to the many and many hearts joined in the One. It is a quantum thing! We use words to go beyond words and sounds to go beyond sounds to embrace the simple realization that "I AM."

Focusing upon the I AM Presence in our daily lives gives us access to our I AM above us, our inner God-Self that is not, and never was, separate from our creator. The more focus and contact we have the more creative and fulfilling our lives become.

Brian Robert's *I AM Presence* book, and his 12-guided mediations are examples of how to invoke the I AM. Both are available on Amazon books.

The 12-minute "I AM" meditation is available for FREE download at: http://Lifeseed-Codes.com

"May all beings be happy, free from suffering, free from enmity, disease, grief, free of troubles, danger, difficulties, and be protected from all misfortune."

Buddhist prayer

First Religion, then Spirituality, then Mysticism and, now this, Letting Go and Letting God

Ever since I stumbled on a book by Mathew Fox that presented commentaries by Meister Eckhart, I can tell Christian people that "oh yeah, I am a Christian" too. Of course, we are probably talking about very different systems. Belief is important to most people. Faith to many others. And then there is the emptiness and the pure light. The Buddha never spoke about God. Jesus is said to have said that the Father within him was the One doing all the good works. The transition from belief to being is an exciting ride. And it takes faith to stay excited about not knowing and giving the whole thing a rest. In other words, you do not have to wrap your head around any idea, concept, or denomination if you can Let Go and Let God. Some Buddhist sects say, "Only don't know."

Meister Eckhart was brought up by the Office of the Inquisition in the early 1300's for speaking truth to power and almost lost his head. He died shortly thereafter, and his writings had to go underground for almost 700 years. I think if I said that he said that a church is a great place to find community but the only place to find God is within, within oneself, he may have said I was interpreting him pretty well. The organization and hierarchy have always wanted to place a dependency upon itself. The priestcraft is crafty. The sometimes- fatal flaw of having to believe becomes the sword of division and domination, which separates us. It keeps us at war with one another and anyone who is at war with another is already at war with him or herself. Some say we are entering the I AM age and awakening!

Did you know that a chimpanzee and a human have 94% common DNA? The difference between us as humans is a .01% difference. That means that you and I are 99.99% alike. That is truly amazing now isn't it? We are all carved out of the same substance and except for this outer coating we are inwardly almost identical. So yes, I am a Christian and a Buddhist and a Taoist, and a Hindu, and a Muslim. I have a profound respect for every reverence for God. The only true religion is the worship of God. The only true spirituality is the total love of God. The only true mysticism is the merging with God. The only discipline is to continue to let go and let God. I have stopped having a plan for my life. Instead, I apply an awareness of preparedness, a relaxed sense of being present in awareness and letting go. No form of belief just an emptiness of flow and function. No intention to mention just a response to guidance within. Letting go and letting God works 100% of the time.

I have an in-law who says I am full of foolishness and there is no God. I laughed and said, "Oh yeah, well what is that that you are breathing just now?" Air and breath, a most amazing way for the presence of God to be both present and invisible. If you do not believe, stop breathing and see the result. Or you could just take a big breath and then just "let go." And be ye divinely guided.

Hakomi – Body-Centered Psychotherapy
Diamond Heart Energy Activations
and a little personal history

In John Denver's song, Rocky Mountain High, he sings, "I was born in the summer of my 27th year, coming home to a place where I've never been before." In the summer of my 27th year, I pulled into Pearl Street in Boulder, Colorado on route to a training in Montana. I never left Boulder; instead, I followed the flow after seeing one of Ron Kurtz's flyers on a telephone pole on Pearl Street. I called Ron and was invited over to his home where he proceeded to encourage me to participate in his training schedule for the summer, in the Hakomi Method. He was also kind enough to offer me a room for the summer. That was the summer of 1980 and the Hakomi method book had just been born.

Ron was a maverick and a synthesizer. Last year, in 2016, they celebrated a Global Hakomi Day. That is how powerful his influence was. Boulder in 1980 was the place to be. The Naropa Institute was there, the Rolf Institute was there, there were Zen Centers, Sufi study houses, macrobiotic study centers, and, not to forget, Hanna Kroger, a famous dowser and nutritionist who lived there. She had her church and health food store there. The community tables at the local restaurants were great places to meet new people. Saturday night the Pearl Street Mall was full of musicians, mime artists, jugglers, crafts people, and other performers. Boulder was perfect for Hakomi work because Hakomi was about to change the way people engaged one another about psychology, therapy, and transformation. Psychology as a science was being introduced to concepts from Taoism and Buddhism, to ideals such as non-violence, love, and compassion. Ron once said about working with clients, "you need to find something to love about them," I believe that was a first in a therapeutic environment. As a rule, the patient/client relationship was one where plenty of padding was applied. The body sciences, massage, deep tissue, Rolfing, Alexander work, had to change all that, and we bodyworkers had to get savvy, be prepared for what was evolving, for what was evolving us. I personally trained for 5 years in a variety of bodywork disciplines before engaging with Hakomi.

One thing that separated Hakomi from most all other therapeutic approaches was that it utilized the body. But most importantly, "we never told anyone what to do, we never gave advice in any form, we never told anyone what we thought their problem was." When you work with the innate intelligence or the collective unconscious, you trust the process, honor the person, hold sacred the journey, and establish a womb-like condition for a person to engage and discover within themselves greater self-awareness, healing and self-sustaining strategies for their own evolution.

This is non-polarizing. It was not about just the client and practitioner. It was about the client, practitioner, and this wonderful thing called, the Unconscious, the Innate, the Field, the I AM Presence, or Source energy. We aligned with that. We had faith, encouraged and practiced mindfulness, developed patience, became insightful and occasionally witnessed some true magic. In other words, we never told people what to do, what to think, or what to believe. We always held these protocols sacred. These ideals and principles are what truly makes these systems of healing holistic. We honor the spirit. We invoke the spirit. We transcend any ego agenda. We practice non-interference. We practice in mindfulness. We stay clear of karma by not injecting ourselves in any way shape or form into another person's relationship to themselves.

Ron passed away a few years ago, and when they were holding a memorial service for him in Ashland, Oregon, I was doing my first public Diamond Heart Energy Activation (DHEA) workshop. If it were not for Ron, I am not sure that I would be doing what I am doing today. When I completed with Hakomi and moved on, I was not sure what the universe had in store for me. I loved Ron, I loved Hakomi, but when Ron headed west, and I headed south and began teaching at the Gainesville School of Massage, our paths parted. I fulfilled on quite a few more post-Hakomi studies, I would graduate the seminary of the Church of Ageless Wisdom, followed by spending 4½ years working in Flo Motion movement research and producing a television show on Flo Motion movement awareness. I lived in five different states for the Flo and that project.

Unfortunately, our Flo Motion infomercial tanked as a result of the Gulf Crisis, so I went into the study of hypnotherapy for both personal and professional reasons. One week before a year of personal sessions and months of training, I experienced my first Alphabiotic alignment. Soon after that, I enrolled in the Alphabiotic training program, received my certification, and opened the Chalice Wellness Center in Seattle. During the 10 years spent there, I performed over 1,000 ceremonies, ordinations, initiations, weddings, christenings, and memorials services.

At this point, I began studying meditation in earnest with Bija meditation, a form of T.M. or mantra meditation. I trained for two years and then went to Thailand for my teacher empowerment initiation into the Council of Light. The self-hypnosis practice of working with oneself two times daily greatly assisted me in beginning a meditation practice. Simultaneously I was studying the LifeWeaving Dowsing System developed by Carole Conlon, a master dowser and teacher. (Her website is AyniLifeWeaving.com). Carole inspired and assisted me in publishing the *Be Clear Now* beginner's dowsing book.

I practiced Alphabiotics for 10 years. After selling that business and moving on, I began studying with many quantum healers, such as Dr. Richard Bartlett's Matrix Energetics and the LightWave with Bryan DeFlores. I picked up the guitar at this point after a 14-year sabbatical, began writing profusely and eventually organized all the music for the Diamond Heart Energy Activations, hereafter referred to as DHEA activations. It seems that pioneers do not sit at the back of the bus. We either drive the bus or ride on the top. All these systems, all these wonderful teachers, have assisted me with their parts into my wholeness. My book *I AM Presence* and accompanying 12 guided meditations is the result of applying the principles of Hakomi, my hypnotherapy training and, most definitely, my work with the Puja ceremony and mantra meditations. There were at least six different systems that I trained in after Hakomi that assisted me in focusing.

With Hakomi, Ron said, "the first thing we do in a therapeutic relationship is to maximize safety and the cooperation of the unconscious. In other words, transformation rarely occurs when two egos are talking. The access for transformation is quantum. The key transformation begins in the open heart. It is in the field or in the self or what I call "the I AM Presence." Master hypnotherapist Dolores Cannon calls it the SC or subconscious, but she clearly redefines this as not the subconscious you have known before. She worked herself into huge spaces, but never changed the name.

In Hakomi, we use or invoke a state of consciousness called mindfulness, which is defined as a distinct state of consciousness. Characterized by relaxed volition, a surrender to and acceptance of the moment. A gentle sustained focus of attention that along with heightened sensitivity is turned inward, towards the Self.

During Diamond Heart Energy Activations, we invite people to lie on a massage table and offer communication with our hands. We energize and balance the chakras. We synchronize the brain hemispheres while listening to a 55-minute guided meditation with visualization, invocations, and mantras for wholeness and healing. I recorded all the music for the activations. And it is free on my lifeseedcodes.com website.

When Ron worked with people, they might go into a big release, hit the floor, and shake a lot; he called this release "riding the rapids." In a six-week training this might happen for five or six people out of 20. His process was awesome, but it took a large amount of time to render. With the DHEA, we muscle tested and calibrated a person's trinity of body, mind, and spirit and very few people tested over 65% integration. After the first session, with DHEA, most participants will reach 90 to 100% integration. Each person requests the download from their own I AM Presence. We practice gentleness, compassion, channeling, and healing. We also do not interfere in people's processes. We do not tell people what to do, what to think, what to believe or how to act. Staying pure and clean as facilitators, we do not practice any karmic exchanges with people. Yes, we do affirm that each of us has Buddha nature. We affirm the absolute probability that each of us will reach Christ Consciousness, and then we get on with the business of getting there.

This is a special process, an evolutionary process. In the years that we have been doing activations, we have observed a sustainable, repeatable execution that has "never failed" to upgrade the energy and percentage of integration of body, mind, and spirit. It will not fix your T.V., computer, cell phone or toaster, but these problems that we have when we function at lower levels of vibration, look totally different to us when we are aligned and balanced. Now they look more like creative challenges to be transformed by us instead. We build character and master the lessons of planet earth. There is a greater consensus with mature individuals that we are in a schoolroom and the best thing to do is put our shoulder to the wheel, the wheel of dharma, even though quite a few people are still throwing stones and adding to the complex dimensions of their personal karma.

Every step up the ladder of our evolution introduces us to a brand-new world. The plan laid out in the Diamond Heart is for 12 unique steps:

    Step One: Body Elemental- Conscious Mind- Super Mind
    Step Two: Communication
    Step Three: Guidance and Intuition
    Step Four: Co Creation, Talents, Productivity
    Step Five: Covenants, Purpose and Plan
    Step Six: Organization and Co Operation
    Step Seven: Synergy and Fluidity
    Step Eight: Self Maintenance, Filtration, Protection
    Step Nine: Grounded in Awareness
    Step Ten: Peace, Power, Prosperity
    Step Eleven: I Dream with Awareness
    Step Twelve: The Returning Point, The Octave, Angel Eyes

Recommendation: if you can do any Hakomi training or personal work such as DHEA, you will be greatly empowered.

Ron Kurtz's book, *The Hakomi Method, Body Centered Psychotherapy*, published by Life Rhythm, is available. I highly recommend it

Footnote: Naropa University is a private liberal arts college in Boulder, Colorado, United States. Founded in 1974 by Tibetan Buddhist teacher Chögyam Trungpa, the school is named for the 11th-century Indian Buddhist sage Naropa, an abbot of Nalanda.

More on Hakomi

I spent a few years in and out of Ron Kurtz's influence and now, some 30 years later, I can see what a great teacher and contributor he was to my life. I can see the principles at work. I can feel the vibration and healing. I wish he were alive today so that I could share my discoveries and activations with him. Although, somehow, I think he is tuned-in and watching over his participants, his flock, from a higher dimension.

Holistic healing must include the spirit if it is going to provide a breakthrough. A new model must emerge. The mind is real, consciousness is real, and it is impossible to know, to see, and to understand all the causes of people's lack of continuity of the body, mind, and spirit.

In our work with the Diamond Heart, the continuity of the body, mind, and spirit is what we hold sacred. Hypnotherapists such as Delores Cannon and even psychiatrists like Dr. Brian L Weiss have both had people during their sessions regress into prior or past lives. This was surprising to both of them as well as to many others. But it has proven to us the past life influence or dynamics of our mental, emotional, physical, and spiritual states. Cannon and Weiss became masters of past life regression.

After years of regression work, Delores said (she passed in 2014) "we don't need to go back there now." Sometimes it may be required, but it is sufficient in today's environment and energies with so many earth changes and vibrational upgrades to work diligently upon staying present and centered in the heart chakra.

I am available to initiate people into the Heart Mantra for meditation and what is easier is this: the Heart Mantra (Hrim) is toned at the end of the 12 minute I AM Meditation. From here, your destiny is yours to decide and impact in a positive way.

The flow of events is never seamless, there are bumps in the road, but there is a metaphysical saying believed by many that "we never get more than we can handle." Where would the world be today if Gandhi was never thrown off the train in South Africa many years ago?

Insight is in-seeing. Execution is skillful means, which originates better from a balanced trinity of body, mind, and spirit. Empowerment is reaching your source point to flow energy for transformation, maintenance, and upgrades.

Integration – in the work, life seeds are planted, nourished, and then harvested.

In the cyclical nature of our life and lives, we learn to follow the processes that deliver the goods, the energy to grow and succeed, to relate, to inspire and be inspired. We begin, we activate, we integrate and then we do it all over again.

As facilitators we do not take credit for another person's success. When successful as participants, we never practice the self-deception of thinking we have already arrived. Instead, we cultivate a fluid and mature attitude of openness, curiosity, and self-inquiry. We continue to work on ourselves.

I personally downloaded the 12 activations from my own I AM Presence. My outer-self, or personality, is still trying to catch up. We can access the Tao of things, we can flow into mindfulness, we can become more I AM centered and, as far as I can tell, the journey always continues.

I am presently working with some form of the activations on a daily basis.

Recommended reading:

Brian L Weiss, MD, *Many Lives, Many Masters*, Simon and Schuster.

Christianity and the Diamond Heart Energy

There is only One River and with just so many streams. I practice mystical or natural Christianity, Inclusive Christianity. I AM especially grateful for the teachings of Meister Eckhart, the 14th century Dominican Christian priest whose work went underground after he was ostracized and exiled in the 1320's. He has probably had the most influence on all world traditions being quoted by the Dali Lama and many Christian leaders alike.

What does that mean to be mystical, natural, and inclusive? Well as far as mystical or natural Christianity is concerned, it involves the practice of meditation to strengthen one's "Source" connections. Translating one's reality through the five senses is one thing. Interpreting one's reality through one's spiritual centers or chakra energy systems is another. The spectrum of consciousness displays different ways of being, of living and of reality, depending on where one is on the scale of consciousness. Plato and Pythagoras were great Christian thinkers who predated Jesus by hundreds of years. Modern meditation practices deliver mystical and natural states of awareness to those who are willing to inquire. Jesus said when "your eye is single your whole body will be filled with light."

Then of course, there are two types of believers. One has true belief and the other has true belief plus wisdom of the truth of this belief. You could say that these two types of belief-holders are like *wavickles*, a term given to light which travels sometimes as a wave and sometimes as a particle. Perhaps a gradual awakening is in the Divine Plan. You cannot really argue with the Divine Plan because if you do, you lose, but only always. Perhaps if we embraced the concept of a gradual awakening, we would all embrace one another? We could fulfill on the request of Jesus for us to love one another even as he has loved us. Powerful!

As a minister I have performed over 1000 ceremonies. Prayers and Invocations are quite natural to me. They can be to *anyone* who wishes to use them, practices them and is empowered by them. Prayer and Silence are most powerful in any tradition, in any church, temple, or organization regardless of the branch or denomination. Light is Light and the bonding light is quite beautiful. The bonding light is that which is God Light, which yields to us and that which is Ourselves, that Will, to bond with Thee, or Unity. All the power that ever was or will be is here now. We use words to transcend words.

Inclusive Christianity is all action and awareness of the activated heart/mind in the domain of all human relationships, activities, and endeavors. It is a service to others, profession, or hobby. A life, filled with love, compassion, ethics, kindness, patience, equality, and joy, is all the same in any language and on any continent, in any time or age. Before the birth of Jesus, Christian ethics were taught in the philosophy of the Tao. The Tao Te Ching has been printed more than any book except for the bible. The Buddha himself never spoke about "God." A humanistic psychology for personal growth and liberation, and for freedom of bondage, pain, mental anxiety and karma, the wheel of dharma turns to liberate souls the Buddhist way. The celebrated Christian monk Brother Thomas Merton recommended that monks and nuns in the Christian tradition would do very well to study the ways and teachings of these ancient traditions especially because of the emphasis on both the "inner way," and meditation practiced by monks worldwide in all traditions.

I once visited with a forest monk in Thailand. Because he missed out registering as a monk, he was in isolation for two years; his monastery was called a Yoga Ashram. These beings have subtle bodies that are so profoundly developed that one easily becomes aware of one's own subtle spiritual bodies while visiting them; healing happens! Since his communication was done largely in silent meditation, the outer name did not matter. I experienced a deep physical shift and healing while simply meditating with him.

In the Hindu tradition there are texts on meditation dating back five thousand years. The Upanishads are teaching inspirational prose that is largely anonymous, predating the Christian era by a thousand years. I have kept a copy of the translation by Juan Mascaro, a Christian Priest, for many years. It says, "Only actions done in God bind not the soul of a man." People have always been inspired to love the Creator, to know the Creator, to serve the Creator. There are a few individuals who live the exemplary life of dedicated service to humanity, also in every culture. Some may say that nature put these people there. Some say God did. I say and pray that we may see more and more of these dedicated integrated ones.

Let's be mystical, let's be inclusive, and let's be ecumenical. Let's swim up the streams and into the river of unity and universality, home to the One. Judgment equals duality, separation, and unnaturalness. Love, kindness, joy, and equanimity equals naturalness, wisdom, and possibility, Be Ye That Possibility of Light. Liberate oneself from the need to be set apart, superior and un-inclusive. Join a higher plan, a spiritual plan, a divine plan, or prosperity plan which starts with us each moment to moment. Take a breath and if you so desire, jump in this river. Your intention will provide the power, your wisdom the direction, your essence the certainty, and your light the love; your destiny is to return home. By the fruits we shall know them.

I AM where I AM in my stream and you are perfect in your stream or river. Like all things that emerge from the One, all things return.

The Law of Attraction

I think it is simple enough to say that everyone is failing or succeeding in the eternal game of the Law of Attraction at every moment, with every moment, in every moment of our lives. That is because it's like gravity. It's all the same all over the planet. Gravity, every moment of every day and nobody ever thinks about it. From the beginning we are told how to focus, what to focus on, what to focus about and what to believe. It is rare to be taught about "how to think." We live in a very belief-based culture and not enough "being" is being celebrated. Take a moment to check in on the pure fact that you do "exist." That's a miracle. We have the power to create, right? Creating is a process of flow from a deeper part of the self/mind/being. Nothing trumps the relationship of you to You, which is your essential, soulful and eternal Self. As a rule, we are very much left in the dark about the truth of the self and although we have many teachers and systems built around metaphysical ideas, many people spend many years reading books and attending seminars and still don't get enough traction to get to where they might like to get in life.

I want to say that I am not an expert on the Law of Attraction, but I do hope to be a good student. Also, I want to share some of my impressions with that intelligence which is called Abraham. I think that that intelligence which is called Abraham is powerful and is offering great wisdom. I have read the Law of Attraction books many years ago and now recently, I have been watching the videos and really have appreciated the dialogues that people have with Abraham. The conversation is the wisdom school, and many options are offered on how to look at situations, possible solutions to the challenges we face today. The kindness, respect and, many times, the deep enlightenment flowing is hard to match in almost any of today's teachers.

The concept on the dynamics of mind have been brought forth by so many new thought teachers, but the interchange through Ester Hicks brings a powerful dynamic. The "hot seat" where people bring "their stuff" to offer to Abraham and the group deepens the inquiry and clear and decisive options are openly discussed. The expanded and enlightened premise that we are that "source energy" on a journey of co-creation, truly appeals to me. As people move beyond religion and into spirituality, we are collectively opening to a larger conversation that embraces more space and possibility. The all-important focus prescribed is that our personal "you" connects with the "non-physical you" and that this awakening energizes our thoughts, dreams, our health, and wellbeing. This connection is the big one. This Self is the one of wisdom and wonder. Maintaining this "source" connection is the way to the path of deliberate intent.

I personally have been in metaphysics for 40 years and have been with many teachers. There is a considerable amount of unwholesome materials generated in many camps. I personally had to move on from quite a few; too many to mention. In the Abraham experience this does not seem to be the case. There is nothing to join and the responsibilities for one's own creations stays with each of us. In the Diamond Heart Energy Activations, we require participants to sign a release form indicating that we are not requiring anyone to sign up, join up, anti-up or re-up. Activations are generated out of an understanding that ALL participants share in the co-creation. We are moving towards a collective understanding about the "I AM Age" and this is generating new and wholesome ways of participation in teachings for spiritual unfoldment. We are beginning to see the difference in the inward-directed processes from the "give it that old time religion" based in belief, and far from experience. A great mystic once said to go to church on Sunday but go to God every day. I am not sure we understand just how pervasive the attending paradigms are and how they affect each and every one of us.

In the teachings of Abraham, they say "There is no point of view, or issue for that matter, that we desire to guide you towards or away from." It is only our desire that you find a way to come into alignment with YOU. For when you do your own life and that world reflects the balance, and, until you do, there is not enough action in the world that can compensate for the misalignments of energy. The Law of Attraction clarifies our understanding that if you want something to happen you need to Ask, Seek and Knock. We need to become a vibrational match to our desires. If you want something, but you do not believe it can happen, then it probably is not going to happen. Then one is proving that the Law is working, only it is working against you (us). Not really, it is always working "for" you (us), but we are not conscious of the way it does.

We are "source energy" and have signed on for a journey of co-creation. There is no hell unless you want to make one up. But then again, there is no heaven if we are continuing to energize our suffering, distractions, stories, and bad karma. The way out is up. Up into a clear and functional awareness about just how powerful and magnetic our beings are, just how powerful our thoughts and emotions are. Our emotions are our guidance system, but only working for us when we are functioning in harmony and balance. Affirmations are good tools for mind training. Prayers and invocations can also be helpful.

Finding a positive thought when we are challenged by daily dynamics is key. We must maintain our dynamic energy center, our vortex, our power, always and under all conditions; this is training and reorientation that is the master path. It is my experience that it is a lonely highway that few people travel, but eventually everyone is going to have to get with the program.

The Law of Attraction was defined in Madam Blavatsky's work as far back as 1887. The absolute best material I have discovered on this subject shows up in *The Master Key System* by Charles F. Haanel. I purchased a hardback edition from Abe books for $1. His book consists of 24 chapters, which are more like lessons that are approached on a weekly basis. Each lesson consists of just a few pages with instructions for specific meditations that begin to connect the conscious and subconscious mind in the most dynamic way. Anyone who has been doing any meditation of any kind will have no difficulty jumping right into this masterful work, which was first published in 1910. Charles says that "Mind is creative, and all conditions, environments and all experiences in life are the result of our habitual or predominant mental attitude." The attitude of mind necessarily depends upon what we think. Therefore, the "SECRET" of all power, all achievement, and all possession, depends on one's method of thinking.

I am convinced that having studied many wonderful authors and teachers for over 40 years, that *The Master Key System* is the best resource I have found on the subject. Therefore, it is not necessary to carry on much further except to say that I highly recommend this book as well as the Ester Hicks' YouTube material. It is often a thing of exquisite beauty to watch the interchange of Abraham and the folks in the hot seat.

People that gather for the purpose of co-creation generate gigantic force fields of light that honor the giver and receiver as equal partners in the miracle of life. It is a good thing to think about Jesus, but it's a better thing to think like Jesus because this is the true inheritance from the creator. This is the gift of co-creation and the understanding of the Law of Attraction is the key to the kingdom.

Key Disciplines

"If you will make the determination that, from wherever you stand and no matter what you are focusing upon, you will reach for the best feeling thought you can find from where you are, then you will develop an ongoing relationship with your INNER

BEING, with Source, and with all that you desire, your life will become consistently joyous."

From the Vortex, Ester and Jerry Hicks, page 24

Key Breakthroughs

I truly hope that someday I can quote Charles Haanel like some people quote the Bible. His work is so very potent. In Chapter 4, line 6, Charles gives us this instruction as follows: "The trained mind knows that every transaction must benefit every person who is in anyway connected to the transaction, and any attempt to profit by weakness, ignorance or necessity of another will inevitability operate to his disadvantage."

4: 7, states: "This is because the individual is a part of the universal. A part of the universal cannot antagonize any other part, but, on the contrary, the welfare of each part depends upon the recognition of the interest of the whole."

4: 8, states, "Those who recognize this principle have a great advantage in the affairs of life."

I will leave you to inquire more deeply into the secret of the Law of Attraction when you begin to take up the training in "The Master Key System" by Charles Haanel or any other number of great teachers on the subject of The Law of Attraction.

States of Consciousness Diagram

A Map of Intrapersonal, Extrapersonal, and Transpersonal Consciousness
Seven Major Levels of Consciousness, Substance, and Energy

Physical matter exists on a continuum with spirit. Thus, matter may be considered to be the densest form of spirit, or conversely, spirit may be considered to be the subtlest form of matter. The Indian sage Sri Aurobindo similarly said that every *prakriti* (substance) has its *purusha* (subtle essence or soul) and, further, that each purusha is in turn a prakriti in relation to a yet subtler purusha. In other words, behind each form is a subtle essence, and behind that is a progression of yet-subtler essences, *ad infinitum*.

From this perspective, the terms *matter, energy,* and *spirit* refer to a single continuum, and may be considered interchangeable. This parallels the concept in modern physics that matter and energy are equivalent and exist on a spectrum of energies that range from low to high frequency.

Hinduism similarly teaches that all manifestations, physical and non-physical, are manifestations of mind. From this perspective, mind or consciousness is equivalent to both energy and matter.

From an esoteric perspective there is a spectrum of seven levels of consciousness/substance/energy. These range from the densest, which is the physical/etheric level, to the subtlest, which are levels of spirit. These seven levels are mapped in the accompanying States of Consciousness Diagram. Each of the seven levels, labeled E1 to E7 in the diagram, may be subdivided into seven sublevels. E1 to E7 are levels of energy/substance/consciousness within both the microcosm – the individual – and the macrocosm.

Though E7 is higher on the diagram than E1, it is important to remember that "higher" on the diagram is not a geographic concept; it does not describe an altitude or a place. Instead, "higher" is a metaphor for subtler. All the states of consciousness/energy/substance represented as Levels on the diagram coexist and intermingle with each other. They are inherent in one another and inseparable.

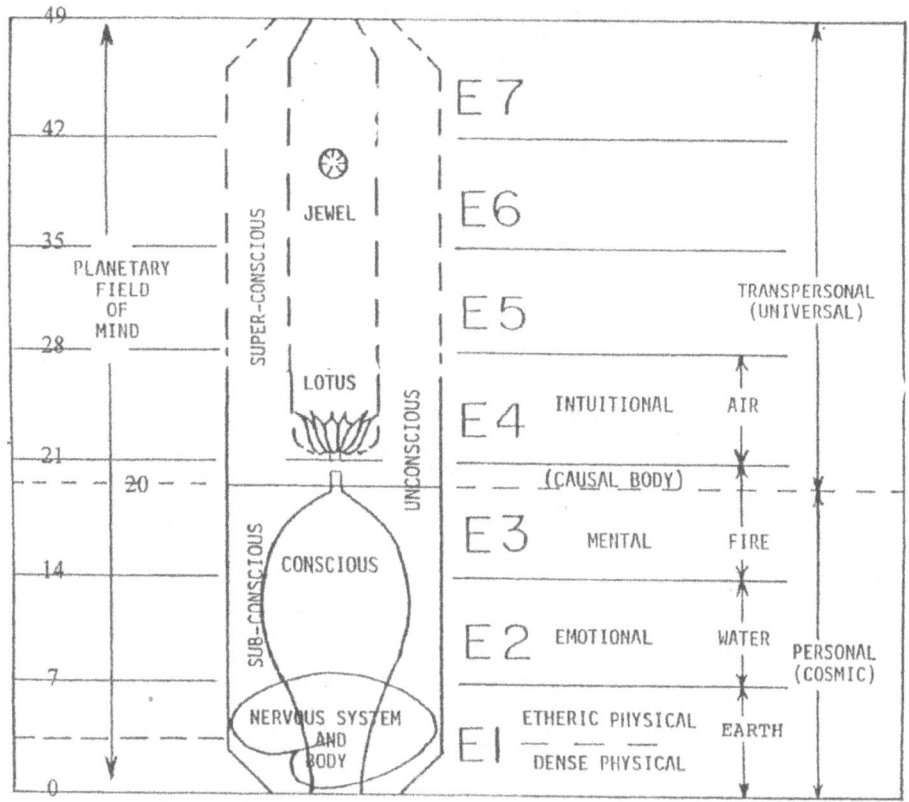

States of Consciousness Diagram

Details of the Seven Levels of Consciousness, Substance, and Energy

Level E1 is the physical/etheric level. Within the physical/etheric realm the densest three sublevels are the solid, liquid, and gaseous phases of matter. Subtler than, or "above," physical matter in the diagram are what are known as the four ethers. The densest ether is ordinary electricity. The other ethers are various forms of subtle energy, also known by such names as *prana* or *chi*. The four ethers may be referred to as either etheric energy or etheric substance, since energy is a form of substance, and substance is a form of energy.

The etheric substance, known as electricity, consists of electrons, and electrons are an inherent component of the atoms that comprise physical substance. Likewise, the three subtler forms of etheric energy are inherent components of physical substance and, under normal conditions, etheric energy is inseparable from physical substance.

E2, the next major level, is emotional substance. This level is also called the astral level. The substances/energies of Levels E2 to E7 are as real as physical substance, though less dense. While we think of emotions as insubstantial, we easily feel them in our bodies as well as feeling them psychologically; thus, they have physical manifestations which we easily perceive. Seers who are sensitive to etheric, emotional, and mental energies can experience them synesthetically as having visual form, or can feel them kinesthetically as heat, cold, vibration, or as a field that is palpable in much the same way that static electricity can be felt as a palpable field.

The seven sublevels of E2 vary from extremely unrefined to extremely refined, sublime emotions. The lowest and most coarse emotional realm is Hell. The highest astral sublevel has heavenly characteristics and is one in the hierarchy of seven heavens in the Kabbalah, but it is much less refined than the ultimate heaven.

Level E3 is the level of mental substance. Thoughtforms exist in this realm and are made of mental substance or energy. The highest sublevels of E3 correspond with highly refined and subtle mental states. Advanced mathematicians and physicists tune into these levels in their work.

The third highest mental sublevel is a level of abstract and creative thinking for figuring out how to do things that are known, such as how to write a novel, create a business, or design a bridge. It is a Thomas Edison-like level of abstract mind and creation.

The second highest mental sublevel is the realm of grand master chess players, theoretical mathematicians and physicists, creators of that which never has come before, innovators who materialize visualizations. It is a rarefied, Nicola Tesla-like level of abstract mind and creation.

Within an individual, the highest and subtlest mental level is the so-called High Self. It serves as the bridge or intermediary between the personal levels of the individual and the transpersonal or spiritual levels.

Levels E1 to E3, being the physical, emotional, and mental levels of reality, are the realm in which the personal self exists. The personal self is an aggregate of physical, emotional, and mental elements; it is literally made of E1 to E3 substances.

That which exists at E1 to E3 is subject to change and is not permanent. Thus, the physical-emotional-mental aggregation that is the personal self is mortal. After death of the body, the soul finds itself in the astral or astral-mental realm. In Tibetan Buddhism, this after-death realm is called the *bardo*. The bardo consists of many gradations or densities of emotional and mental substance into which the soul metaphorically "rises" like a balloon until it reaches that level of the Earth's emotional-mental milieu. This corresponds with the density or subtlety of the soul's emotions and thoughts, conscious and unconscious, during its just-completed life on earth.

In contrast to E1 to E3, Levels E4 to E7 are increasingly subtle levels of spirit. They are thus transpersonal. They correspond with Heaven. In Hinduism and the Western esoteric tradition, the transpersonal aspects of the self are considered the True Self.

That which exists at transpersonal levels is beyond the realm of time and change and is eternal. ("Eternal" is a tricky concept here. It does not mean lasting forever since this is a state that is beyond time. "Without beginning or end" is closer to being accurate. It would also be relatively correct to simply say about this level that "I Am," or "It Is" rather than saying that "It is eternal.")

The Cosmos

Levels E1 to E3 are comprised of the substances – physical, emotional, and mental – of which the personal self, the microcosm, is made. From an esoteric perspective, the macrocosm – the cosmos, the known universe – is composed of the same three types of substance. Inherent within physical substance are astral and mental levels of energy/substance. Thus, the esoteric "cosmos" includes more than the physicists' cosmos, which is only physical, E1.

The entire spectrum from E1 through E7 constitutes "all that is. Elmer Green refers to this totality as the *kosmos*. The cosmos includes the levels of reality within which the microcosm, the personal self, exists. In contrast, Dr. Green's term kosmos includes both personal and transpersonal levels.

In Tibetan Buddhism, the personal level, E1 to E3, is the realm of the four bardos: the bardo during birth, the bardo during life, the bardo during dying, and the bardo after death or between incarnations. Again, the bardos are equal to the personal or cosmic levels of reality, while spiritual levels are transpersonal, transcosmic, and transbardo.

Dream consciousness, the collective unconscious, and the after-death bardo are all unconscious realms; that is, outside of ordinary waking awareness. These three terms describe approximately the same realms of consciousness, occupying the same territory on the Diagram. Dreams may potentially occur on any level of consciousness, personal or transpersonal, though most dreams concern personal issues and thus focus on the personal levels of the diagram, E1 to E3. Likewise, the collective unconscious includes all seven levels of the diagram; however the levels of it which an individual may glimpse will tend to correlate with the level of consciousness to which they have developed, again personal for most people. Meanwhile, the after death bardo is the portion of the collective unconscious at the personal levels, E1 to E3. The after-death bardo is mainly centered on the astral realm.

By definition, since the bardo is the personal realm, and since fully enlightened individuals have developed to transpersonal levels, the consciousness of such individuals is not "in" the bardo after death, i.e., their consciousness is not focused in the personal/bardo realms after death. Instead, their consciousness is focused on Level E4 or higher.

The Boundaries of the Personal Self and Conscious Awareness

In the States of Consciousness Diagram, the individual is represented by the cylinder that runs from top to bottom in the middle of the diagram. Levels E1 to E7 are the Kosmic *ground* within which the individual.

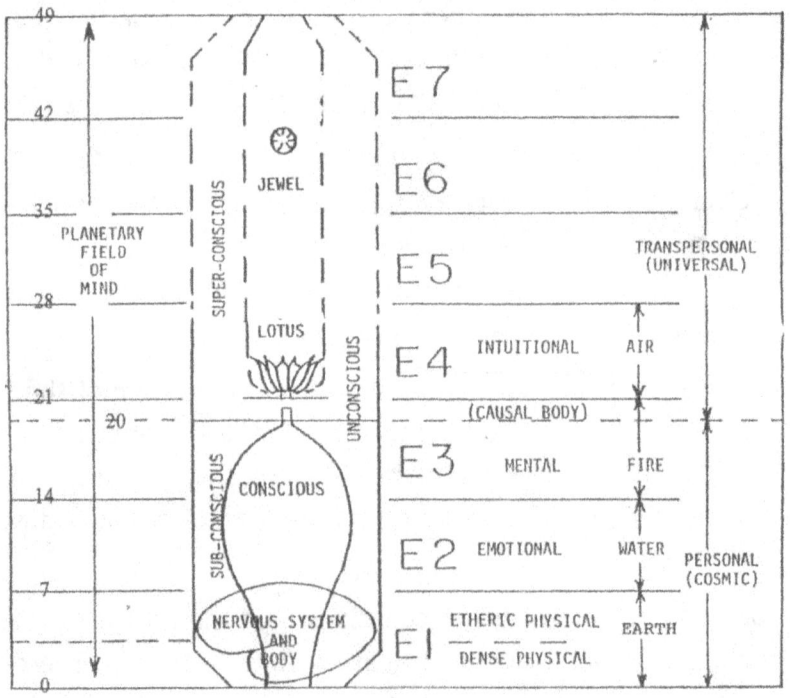

States of Consciousness Diagram

Near the bottom of the cylinder, the diagram shows a drawing of a brain. Because the brain is a physical structure, it is drawn entirely within the physical level, E1. Partly superimposed on the drawing of the brain is a structure that is shaped vaguely like a light bulb. This represents the approximate boundaries of conscious awareness in a typical human. Conscious awareness is drawn as narrower at the physical level, since we are unaware of much of what goes on in our bodies. It is wider at the emotional and mental levels, where we normally tend to be more consciously aware. The area of the diagram outside the light bulb shape represents that which is outside of conscious awareness (for most people). The macrocosm, which is outside the individual cylinder, and the spiritual levels of the individual are outside of ordinary conscious awareness. Though the brain may be considered the seat of consciousness, we are unconscious of the substance of the brain itself, thus the area of conscious awareness overlapping the brain on the diagram is small.

Porous Ego Boundaries Allow Perception of Extrapersonal Information

The ego or personality may be defined as that which separates the individual from the environment. The diagram represents this separation of self from non-self with solid lines in the wall of the cylinder at the personal levels of the diagram, E1 to E3. The solid lines symbolize the fact that, under ordinary circumstances at least, extrapersonal information does not cross the boundary of the ego or personality. Individuals are aware of what is in their own minds and bodies but are not psychically aware of what is in the minds and bodies of others, nor aware of information from distant locations in the world. (Paranormal perceptions such as subtle energy awareness, ESP, or clairvoyance are exceptions to this. Individuals with such perceptual ability would be represented on the diagram with breaks in the lines of the cylinder at personal levels. Such breaks would be few or many, depending on the degree of paranormal awareness.)

At transpersonal levels, the walls of the cylinder are drawn with broken lines symbolizing that a separate self does not exist at those levels and that, in the absence of ordinary ego boundaries, information can be exchanged. Thus, if a person is developed to the Lotus Level within E4, i.e., is fully enlightened, they might have extrasensory awarenesses about their environment or other people.

Of people who are not enlightened, a percentage have gaps in their ego boundaries for a variety of reasons. As a result, they may perceive extrapersonal information including, for example, emotions of other people or experiences of "the other side" or the bardo. This can potentially occur in cases of:

- psychologically healthy people who happen to be psychic
- some people who practice certain forms of meditation
- people with brain deterioration due to dementia
- people with serious physical illnesses of many kinds which compromise brain function
- people under the influence of mind-altering drugs
- people with psychosis, which is a decompensation of ego boundaries
- people whose ego boundaries are incompletely developed, as in autism or severe personality disorders

The High Self

The High Self exists at Level 21, the highest mental level and the highest of the personal sublevels. The High Self correlates with the Son in the Christian Trinity. Though technically within the personal realm, the High Self is refined enough that its energies or communications typically seem to the ego to be spiritual in nature. People may interpret such input as being from God. The High Self's function is, in part, that of guardian angel of the personality. High Self energy is associated with the seventh chakra, at the crown of the head.

Causal Levels

Levels 19, 20, and 21 are shown on the diagram as "Causal," meaning that they cause manifestations at lower levels. Specifically, incarnation into levels E1 to E3 is stimulated from the causal levels. The *skandhas*, which are the reservoirs of personal characteristics that are transmitted from one incarnation to the next, exist at the causal levels. In the same way that physical DNA encodes and carries physical characteristics from one generation to the next, the *skandhas* act as "spiritual DNA," transmitting certain personal characteristics from one incarnation to the next.

The Antahkarana and the Abyss

The diagram shows a narrow channel at Level 21, at the top of the bulb-shaped conscious awareness. Above this is a gap, and above the gap is the Lotus (rep presented in the diagram as a lotus flower below the word "LOTUS"). The narrow channel represents the *antahkarana* which, in Hinduism, is a metaphoric conduit through which spirit connects with the ego. The *antahkarana* is within the levels of the ego, rather than being transpersonal. It is symbolized in Genesis as Jacob's ladder, which connected heaven and earth. In dreams, the *antahkarana* may be represented as a narrow passageway or a dark interior space through which the dreamer ascends, emerging through an opening at the top into light. The dreamer may emerge onto the top of a structure, such as a building, and there may be no means of going higher. This represents the furthest upper limit of the personal self. The story of Marty in *The Ozawkie Book of the Dead* describes a dream containing *antahkarana* symbolism.

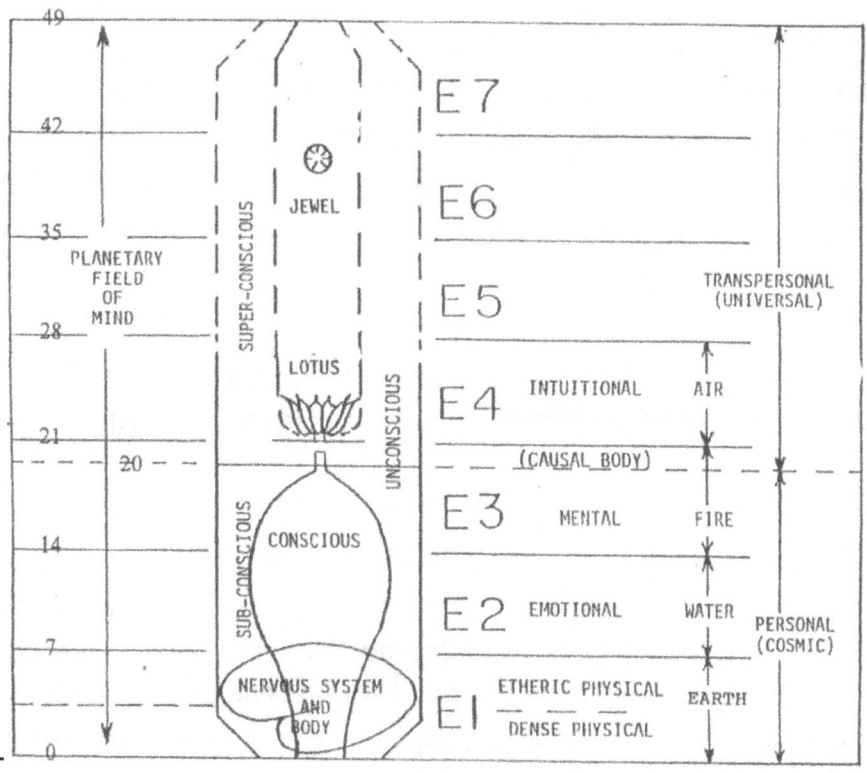

States of Consciousness Diagram

Though an ego focused at this highest mental level is highly developed and refined, it may seem to the ego that an unbridgeable gap exists between itself and spiritual levels. This gap is shown on the diagram between the *antahkarana* and the Lotus.

The gap is sometimes referred to esoterically as "the Abyss." The word abyss means an unfathomable gap or immeasurably deep gulf. In dreams the abyss may be represented as some form of gap or expanse which appears too formidable to be crossed (until the individual has further developed spiritually). Elmer Green's dream of the swans contains imagery of an abyss which he and Alyce are able to cross.

The Lotus

At the spiritual levels of the individual are two foci, the Lotus and the Jewel. These terms are drawn from the Tibetan Buddhist and Hindu traditions, which refer to them in the widely known phrase *Om, Mani Padme Hum* (which is often translated as Hail to the Jewel in the Lotus). Great teachers who have achieved full enlightenment, that is, who have released all physical, emotional, and mental attachments, have their locus of consciousness at the level of the Lotus.

Being unattached to that which is personal, enlightened individuals are able to manifest their personality at any moment when it is needed to interact but can voluntarily drop the persona at other times.

Lotus consciousness, while impersonal, is a locus of unconditional love and compassion. In the Kabbalah it correlates with the Seventh Heaven, known as the "Heaven of Heavens." Lotus energy is transmitted through the eighth chakra, which is located above the head.

The Lotus is located at Level 22 in the diagram, the lowest sublevel of the transpersonal realms. It may be thought of as the spirit behind the High Self.

The Jewel

The spirit behind the Lotus is the Jewel, located at Level 42, the highest sublevel of E6. It is also known by the Western term *monad*. While the Lotus is a locus of unconditional love, the Jewel is a locus of spiritual will. Its energy is transmitted through the ninth chakra which is located above the head, above the eighth chakra.

TransKosmic Levels

According to teachers whom Sri Aurobindo consulted, there is an infinite progression of levels of consciousness/energy/substance beyond E7. Teachers or spiritual forces/entities above E7 are so subtle that they are not able to contact the human realm, that is, the Kosmos. Levels beyond E7 are TransKosmic and are not shown on the Diagram.

The author wishes to acknowledge Dr. Elmer Green for his contribution, article, and diagram of the *States on Consciousness, A Map of Interpersonal, Extrapersonal and Transpersonal Consciousness*. Used with permission from his Trust.

PART FOUR

PROSE, POEMS AND ALMOST ZEN KOANS

CHAPTER 9

Introduction to Prose, Poems, and Almost Zen Koans

All creativity results from contact with your I AM Presence. Your I AM is the God aspect within. Everyone is joined in this sacred reality of spirit, on some level, and then there is the planet Earth on the third dimension of life. Here, something else is happening. Most of us are unable to hear the angels singing. Therefore, we must make an effort to "wake up."

This effort here with Prose, Poems and Almost Zen Koan is an effort to share humor, inspiration, and meditations for this purpose. My other two books really require a commitment, an effort in order to wrap one's head around the material. Here, I AM sharing some poems and thoughts because they seem to have a life all their own. I will often write something, which may be abstract to me, and then someone contacts me, and it appears they need the message. The poem "The Wind Whispered Mary" was very much like this.

Also, I believe that I AM on a journey of service in this life, in an effort to fulfill my obligation I try to make accessible to other travelers, methods for establishing clarity, contact and cohesion. Perhaps this inspiration will continue to flow.

A Life Seed Code Poem

Taking a breath into the new fresh space
Within my heart a wholesome place
Now that the freedom bells have rung
New mantras to sing and songs to be sung
No need to save the world anymore
Or crawl down the street knocking on doors
At home in the heart one can see the whole world
A journey of a thousand miles without moving an inch
I love it
I Ask, I Seek, I Knock and still muscles have not stirred
The Still Small Voice uttered not a word
There is pause right there between each and every breath
I AM here in this place of knowingness
It's blessed
It's new; it's fresh and delicious
So what's the deal, it is true and it is real
No picture of Jesus on the wall
Can't find the Buddha anywhere at all
And yet everything is right as rain
As right as rain

Explanation: I have been a student of ascension philosophy since the early 90's. Many of us were wondering what was happening back then. There were comets coming through the sky and plenty of talk about the close of the Mayan calendar. Although, I have mentioned in my books that planet Earth has become an initiation chamber, I had no idea that the upgrades would continue with such frequency and intensity, now well past December 21, 2012. In the January *Quantum Awakening* newsletter, a short article called the Messiah Code, by Gillian Macbeth-Louthan, inspired this poem. I contacted her after I read her Messiah Code and explained that since the winter solstice of 2018, I felt like I had a vacuum cleaner attached to my crown chakra. It was intense. As I write this, I AM only 36 hours past the Wolf Blood Moon eclipse of January 21, 2019. The energies are still very intense.

Now something has shifted for me and I feel that I AM, or it is translating more smoothly as I Ask, Seek and Knock in a new way. In service to other people the one common mistake we often make is giving in a diminishing way. The quantum energies that are downloading into all of us collectively seem to be anointing us from inside out. The notes, tones and rhythms of this cosmic symphony beg to be simply indulged and resonated. They are free energies that are not asking us to sign up with any directives or restraints. Our simple, humble presence sitting at the feet of the Holy One in any form of God or Goddess or open sky, completes the circuit. I was awakened a week ago from a dream where liquid crystals were being placed inside me. They appeared to be seed crystals. When I planted some, they took the forms of my desire, amazing gardens, and structures of light.

I hope that this poem will light a fire in you and confirm what you already know: that the kingdom is within each and every one of us. We can meet the Buddha and Jesus on the road and embrace in unity and equality. Or we can walk alone. We can take down the pictures on our walls past and open now the windows of spirit in celebration, plain and simple.

Go ahead read the poem again and let it really sink in.

Blessings,
Brian Timothy Roberts
January 23, 2019

Again and Again

The closer you come to Caesar, the greatest the fear
The closer you come to Jesus, the opposite is true
It's all well-designed plan, the Buddha is great too
It's all in the Divine Plan, with its colors of green,
of gold and of blue
Rest yourself in that One Divine Breath
That will raise your attitude too
A rainbow bridge, with starts moving all around my feet
I wonder if my journey will soon be complete
Never says the whisper of the wind
It's only always just time to begin
Again and again

I AM

I Believe
I believe in God
I believe in the Oneness of God
I believe in the Absolute Love of God
I believe in the God on my being
I believe in the God of all being
I believe in the God beyond our belief
I believe in the One God with all my being
I believe in the God beyond my being
I believe in the One God of Grace
I believe in the One God of All time and All space
I believe I AM grateful to exist in this place.
I believe for myself and for all sentient beings.
The holiness of the awareness of silent mindful breathing
Opens
And then
Emptiness
Is

Gazing into the Freedom Mirror

Remember to focus your lenses of forgiveness
Vibrate the healing power of love.
Let gratitude be your attitude in awareness.
Accepting a flow of light from above.
Breathe this in and around yourself,
In rhythm like sounds and the beats of the Earth,
We are grounded in.
Invoking the wisdom from all of the ages.
Each moment of being our being is birthed.
Moment by moment and breath by breath
One climbs the ladder magnificent.
Existence adorns each atom and electron.
On the long lovely journey in light we are sent.
Now gazing into the mirror, the mirror of wonder
Once again and as free citizens.
Free to be,
To simply just Be

Milestones and Gemstones

It is easy to recognize gemstones when you see them
They sparkle and shine and have a life force associated with them
The soul has a schedule with its evolution and along the way the milestones which it passes and achieves are subtle for the seeing, but oh so freeing
It is not easy being an evolving being on the planet right now.
And some say this is the greatest time to be alive
because the light of the new Earth is beginning to
shine and sparkle
because God is coming to Earth and beginning to walk with man.
And you can see this
A young man assists an old women across the street
God made him do it
A man writes a check for the Boy's club in his neighborhood
His God self made him do it
A women shaves her head and receives initiation and acceptance into the monastery at Mt Shasta
The Goddess made her do it
She becomes enlightened
A milestone, a gemstone
A man and a woman adopt children and exude a love that radiates like a Christ or like the Buddha. They step aside the little self and embrace life, possibility, sacrifice, humility, and love
Milestones and Gemstones

They become the gemstones of the living light of love and pass another milestone on the mountain of life, of evolution,
and of the soul
They listened and responded to the call, and now love has brought them further and further along that long road to enlightenment
That was a milestone
They shine like gemstones
A family is born
Milestones and Gemstones

Now the actions of our lives are powerful seeds that are placed in the vital darkness/light of possibility, in the isolation of sacrifice that births flowers for future fellow travelers to enjoy, on their walk to freedom. You have walked by the fragrant flowers of your ancestors and felt them well. Yours is a journey of milestones and gemstones, blessing those who have gone before you, those who travel with you and those still yet to come,
for Milestones and Gemstones

Mystery and Silence

As the story goes, and whether if it is true or not, is beside the point. Teaching stories are always given to us for the intrinsic value, for the essence, for the life seed codes. Wherever the fertile soil of the heart is, receptive the winds will come, sun will shine, and the birds of love and life will offer the magical and necessary starts for flowering and fruit.

Long, long ago in the late part of the eighth century, in a very remote village in India, by chance (if you can believe in that) a certain Swami Nasrudin, a local tea shop restaurant and food distribution tent owner had attracted the attention of a number of wandering sages, a sadhu, a monk and even one guru. Rarely did this place receive visitors from outside. Now suddenly there were plenty of guests of impeccable character and fortitude. Perhaps it was the 777 Gateway? Who knows, who cares, this is fiction, or is it? So, this gentleman decided after offering some food and tea to these visitors, that some sort of a gathering might be appropriate for the enlightening of the locals and also for the honoring of these radiant, but simple and humble beings.

It was still only in the eighth century, so a little news of the Buddha would be whispered, but most clung to the beliefs of the Hindu Gods such as Vishnu, Brahma, and Shiva. Shankara, the great reformer of spiritual culture and of Vedanta, had not yet appeared on the scene. But even the god's names changed from time to time. There were no statues of the deities or the divine mother, but just earth and sky as far as the eye could see. The people were simple and sweet, without arms and armies, and took the best care of one another. Not having much there was nothing to protect. The children were taught to respect the elders, so all adults were looked upon as aunts and uncles. Songs were sung. Work was done. All was as one might imagine, evolving and moving in the Way and returning to the One.

Occasionally someone would bring one of Confucius' quotes (by most traditional accounts, Confucius around 484 BC spent the remainder of his life teaching, putting in order the *Book of Songs*, the *Book of Documents*, the *I Ching* and other ancient classics). It was not totally foreign at a meeting to hear quotes such as "Ability will never catch up with the demand for it." Or "Choose a job that you love, and you will never have to work a day in your life." And of course, the one everyone knew, "Life and death have a set of predetermined appointments, what comes in the middle is up to you." And of course, there was the quote "The superior man is ALL embracing and not partial, the inferior man is partial and not ALL embracing."

The locals had their own wisdom too, and even at the tent where shoes were made and repaired, a sign read "Real Shoes and No Imitations." And of course, there was this saying, "When you don't know what you ain't got, so what." Signs of simple wisdom were found all around. But more attention was on the shovels and the mules. One humorous sign said, "If your barn is on fire the best way out is the closest door or window." And of course, in the summer you would see signs by the river like "Don't swim upstream, it is hard on your system and there are really cool people down river."

Padmasambhava (considered to be the second Buddha) had not yet been born and had not entered into the hearts and minds of the Indian or Tibetan people with his light, wisdom, or with his declarations that "Awareness is key" and that the ultimate sphere of reality is beyond the senses and that "Non-duality is the home and destiny of all sentient Beings."

The saying that "The Tao that could be told was not the Eternal Tao."

"The name that could be named is not the Eternal name."

"The nameless is the beginning of Heaven and Earth." And the Tao Te Ching was not available at a local bookstore, because there were none. And Lao Tsu had never been heard of even though he was considered a contemporary of Confucius. Today however, and or still, the Tao Te Ching by Lao Tsu has been printed more than any other book except for the bible. Thank God for that! And it shows you how little exposure these simple people really had. No Tao, No How!

Christ had come and gone and left his sign and seal upon the etheric of the planet, but few knew where the ladders and labyrinths of light were accessible. Forgiveness and love sounds a lot like empathy and compassion so all good peoples kept an open heart and mind knowing that the simple, but necessary, activities of farming and cultivation were so central to the way of life that schools of learning would come when they would come, as simple as that, later.

The great mystic poet Mevlana Jalaluddin Rumi was still five hundred years in everyone's future. We would all have to wait for all his poems, quotes and inspiration. Like "Love rests on no foundation, it is an endless ocean without beginning or end."

Rumi said, "I can't stop pointing to the beauty. Every moment and place say, put this design in your carpet."

And "If you are irritated with every rub, how will your mirror be polished?"

And "The minute I heard my first love story I started looking for you, not knowing how blind I was. Lovers don't finally meet somewhere. They are in each other all along."

And although Jesus had told those who had ears to hear, to ask, to seek and to knock, Rumi had a way with words like the wind had whispers for things.

He said and we quote "Knock and he will open the door. Vanish and he will make you shine like the sun. Fall, and he will raise you to the heavens. Become nothing, and he will turn you into everything."

So you could possibly imagine that the guy who was insightful enough to recognize these people in his tent, to see their light, to feel their emanations, to hear the peace and joy which accompanied their speaking was probably an early incarnation of one of the ones who organized the Harmonic Convergence, perhaps the first Live Aid concert. I mean the guy was savvy, had a lot of animals, the biggest tent in the area, a beautiful wife with great beautiful eyes and his beard was not even that long. His sandals looked like an early version of Birkenstocks and it appeared that he was wearing some kind of designer jeans, otherwise humble without a sign of tie-dyed or hippie attire. You remember this is late eighth century, and rural. Lots of stars.but no Starbucks.

Nasrudin was also called the swami because he was a source for things; when a person needs credit you always warm up to those who are extending it! He was really only lucky that when he was born, he was the only male child with lots of females for years, interesting luck some might call it.

So Nasrudin put the word out that some unusual circumstances had come about and that a special evening of discussion, debate and discourses would be going on as his guests would be extending themselves to the community for Satsang or something.

The first guest, a Buddhist monk began to speak most eloquently about Buddhism and why it was the most important development for the liberation of the mind, for the opening of the heart, and for the liberation of the Soul. Every once in a while, he would sing the mantra Om Mani Padme Hum which was so so beautiful.

Having decided that he had made a great contribution and in fact saved many souls and directed those on the *Only True Path to Enlightenment* he humbly bowed down and then sat down on the floor.

Next, the Hindu Brahmin priest began to speak of the ability of the adept to give through grace, the experience of enlightenment to any individual who was sincere. This would be as such a momentary look into the nature of the Self and God and the

Universe. Having had this experience, one then would be taught the Sanatana Dharma or teachings of the Hindus and the Vedas and the Upanishads and be brought eventually into the fullness of self-realization. He concluded with a bow and a promise that this path was the *Only True Path to Total Enlightenment.*

Next, a monk from a Christian monastery began to speak about the Good News of Jesus and the coming of the Kingdom of God. He said that Jesus was the only son of God and the *Only Way to Heaven* was through being washed and bathed in the forgiveness of sins and the power of the Holy Spirit and the Resurrection. He too felt confident that he had come to finally get these folks on the right track to redemption and salvation.

The Buddhist monk looked at the Hindu priest and said, "It is the four-fold noble path that is right and solid."

The Hindu priest said "It is the deepening and experience of the atman, of pure consciousness, of awareness without an object. This is a must for spiritual enlightenment."

The Buddhist monk said no no no. "It is the Eight-Fold Noble Path that purifies the individual for the removal of the samskaras, the illusions, the crap and the karma for liberation."

The Christian monk sat in disbelief thinking didn't they hear a word of the Word? Like JC is the light of the world and the only way to God. They had better listen or the hell fire is going to cook their bodies.

Sat Chit Ananda, the Hindu monk kept repeating and repeating: "Truth, Consciousness, Bliss."

The Buddhist monk now was standing and shouting out "It is the four-noble truths and the eight-fold path." "It is the four-noble truths and the eight-fold path;" "It is the four-noble truths and the eight-fold path."

Sat Chit Ananda, the Hindu monk kept repeating and repeating: "Truth, Consciousness, Bliss."

Finally, one of the guests picked up a large mallet and swung it with tremendous power, hitting a gong that reverberated throughout the tent. I mean it was loud, really loud.

A deep and wonderful silence fell upon the crowd.

A really deep and really wonderful silence fell upon all members of the crowd.

The gong master then stared over at a man of tremendous radiance and peace. He said, "Dear stranger are you a monk, are you a priest, are you guru, are you a shaman, are you a visionary, are you a mystic, are you some kind of a prophet, or just what are you?

And what do you have to say about these here debaters, satsangers, discourses, about taking refuge in the Buddha, or JC is the Only Way, or the four plus eight equals the 12 steps to Nirvana. What, what, what do you think?"

The man was simply alive with joy, with love, with compassion, with vision, his simply standing in the room was a light show of golden and silver light. Waves of energy were radiantly emanating out of his eyes, out of his heart, out of his aura.

He lifted his hands in a gesture of opening, of gentleness and of peace and power and said, "Dear ones, I agree with everything that everyone has said here tonight."

Then he repeated himself saying that he believed everything that everyone has said here tonight, as his eyes scanned the room making deep contact with the monks, the people, and the priest.

A peace fell, descending into the room; a glow precipitated itself. The gong seemed to start to vibrate on its own. Tears fell, hearts sang, minds opened.

How can you believe that all you have heard is correct he was asked?

The questioner scratched his head. How does it make sense?

Each one is allowed his freedom, and the freedom of one's own beliefs. Is this not right? Can you interfere in this? In what a man thinks? I think not! No. Is a man not free to think? And thoughts are just that, thoughts.

He said, "We are all, only always all ways, on the perfect path in the One, from the One and to the One, to liberation, to freedom. Unity is simply always the case.

We are all, only always all ways, on the perfect path in the One, to the One, from the One, to liberation, to freedom. Unity is simply always the case. Continuity is the ground. Light is the substance.

When crossing a lake, he said use a boat. When crossing a mountain use a mule. When you are tired lie down and sleep. When you are hungry eat. When you are thirsty drink. When preparing for winter chop wood. When meditating go deep into the Heart of the Silence. Then words will be words. Thoughts will be thoughts. mantras will be mantras, and the silence that joins all living things will be the silence that joins all living things.

Unity is all ways already the case. Listen, and hear what the silence will tell you!

The only True path there is to take, is the one we are all already on.
The only True path there is to take, is the one we are all already on.

Brian T Roberts
1/3/12

When Gandhi Pours Your Tea

There is hardly any need for sugar when Gandhi pours the tea.
It is a moment of such elegance, that you must simply see.
Ramanana Maharshi would not start to eat until everyone was served.
He was a holy man, a knowledge man
that people came to India from worldwide to observe.
Jesus said that "No greater love hath a man, that he would lay down his life
for his beloveds, his friends".
The Sufi's say that you must kneel in this world to stand in the next.
The bible says that the first shall be last and the last shall be first.
What is the moral, the message,
the transmission in these actions and words?
Love
Loving thy neighbor
Loving thy neighbor as thy Self
Oh what a Self we are
made of God glory.
Of Light, Of Infinity
And service is the key to life.
And if service be the key, for me,
how to go about this most exquisitely.
Properly, humbly, powerfully, and pure
Not casually, or superficially, but with a deep and certain integrity.
As an expression of grace flowing,
Like water returning to the sea,
Like a pink and red setting sun.
ALL TRUE service is done unto the ONE,

God There really is no other.
All spirit is One, you, me, us, as we
as ONE, true being.
Only in the outer darkness does this small shadow cast
a reflection of itself through the distorted looking glass,
of poverty, of extortion, of war.
Release the claim to the death bound littleness, to the ego night.
And have a life. And have a light.
And if you would at last reclaim your divinity
simple as it sounds,
Service is the Key, the open door to get free.
Be the gift that has no giver
except Source
Resonate the celestial sound of life through the empty flute of your being as,
This becomes our course, our destiny, on homeward, and to being free.
Each and every awakened one has this moment you see, of Unity.
And for this awakening experience, service is the key.
To Life, To Light, To Be.
As simplicity, as key.

Cycles

I find a kindness in stillness right now
Movement will return only later
A peace which engages me installs a
Great silence it seems
The sounds that abounds
As planets and suns circle
Their way
Through the dance of the
Light
Will certainly return
Singing and spiraling
In rest I am blessed
The giant self circles above
And mirrors the light
Of our ancient beginnings
A return to source
The new light grids are in place almost
I breathe the air of expected wonder
New bodies of light emerge
New codes and keys
And the dance of eternities
Dawn's
awakening

Blessings

Blessings Be
Blessed Are
Blessed are Thee
Blessed are the Pure
Blessed are the Pure of Heart
Blessed are the Pure of Heart for they shall be
Blessed are the Pure of Heart for they shall be having eyes
Blessed are the Pure of Heart for they shall be having eyes to see
Blessed are the Pure of Heart for they shall have eyes to see the reality
Blessed are the Pure of Heart for they shall have eyes to see the reality of Love
Blessings be upon you this Holy Season of remembering your Source connections
Blessings be upon you this Holy Season of remembering your essential unity with all Life
May this cycle be an Upward Spiral of Color and Love and Light from Above
to Empower that, which always was, always is
and which always will be the
Truth of who we are Eternally
As Love, as Light and as such beautiful frequency,
Remembered in Totality
Blessings for the Christ Consciousness to empower your life for a most auspicious
New Year

Our Mothers

Our Mothers, full of Grace, heaven holds your secrets and splendor
that humility has you waiting to appreciate and to openly realize.
We Bless you and thank you for being and for hearing our call upon the
Holy Winds, where Angels' wings sing, and harps begin our mornings of
remembering.
A secret golden bond is reached even before our dreams of being and beginning can take flight as dreams within you.
Only Mothers wings can fly at these invisible heights in the clear
crystal and blue sky of beauty and creation.
You are tuned secretly and silently to the Divine impulse that
transcends the spoken word.
Only thee can call to be a life so full of all possibility,
and open your
temple so miraculously,
For birth, from heaven to earth.
Where a Divine song and light forms us,
Within your strong arms and bosom of loving protection.
You have heard the far oft promptings of our spirit innocence,
And carried us in your hope and vision, as our whole welcoming
committee.
You have made the impossible possible and given the gift of your very
own blood for it.
Inside your temple are heart strings and receptors that link with the
most high beings of cosmic origin that still sing your praises to God,
listen.

When you give us our bodies, our tiny hands, our feet, you are helping God fulfill
on his/her dreams of being and creating.
They are singing for you even now, close your eyes a minute and remember.
Who? All of heaven who stayed home in the comforts of pillowy clouds,
those who hesitate in this Divine intervention.
Acknowledge the secret God of your cells
with a breath and a smile.
Acknowledge the divinity of your roots.
Look out upon the fields that love being plowed.
Take a moment of essence to enjoy the fruits.
Look past the world and its challenges and realize like you
All things are born of the One Being
And return as love
T'is True

Buddha and Nature

The Buddha is the Buddha because he has discovered

what is natural

He has looked within

He has observed the bare essentials

and somewhere in the process he has loved himself

Free

not the prince

but the King

not just that which is born of the flesh

but that which is born of

non-being

What is this that is born of non-being

This

I'll whisper it again

What is this that is born of non-being

This

Love

Life Seed

The Seed of all things possible lies buried inside of us
the One, the All, the Omniscient, Omnipotent, Omni Present
is sleeping in us and dreaming of vast open spaces
and endless waves of unfathomable bliss

Always & All ways inviting us to rise above
is creating infinitely
maintaining all as perfection

And a stout open heart will find this
and a conscious breath will awaken to this
a focused prayer will take you there
and a patient mind is kindness where
your commitment learns to live with care
and any sense of separation is arrested
a prayer with wings arrives and honored
turns base metal into a golden
vessel shaped like a chalice
as you turn and re-turn in holy spirals
all because you have assigned yourself the task
of acting Divine
in a place where the Sun shines,
but only half the time
Now this is the age where **your** dreams can become refined
Here perfect strangers give you a body and pass on

their limitations freely
and you must thank them and leave them, forgive them, release them.
like a shower of rainbows in the Sun
and when to the silence you have listened
your insides begin to glisten, bright and shiny like opals
and full moon smiles

Long shadows of doubt and of doing without
are gathered under your feet. So,
now that the Sun is over and above,
You awhile,
gather the light with all of your might
as the height of your flight will depend on this

Let all of your circle's be unbroken
your song is on the harp and well sung
now you will once again light the Light
that lights the light that lights our Sun
and your Seeds are planted into the darkness
where you deliver light
Bright and Shiny light
like only you
can.
Seed Light

What was Our Lady Doing When the Angel Came?

She was sitting, a creature, uncreaturely
She was sitting contemplating the One
She was sitting in a time so untimely
She was sitting, her mind was heavenly calm
And I looked and wondered who she was,
the wind whispered Mary

She was sitting with a heart aflame in living truth
She was sitting in her life altogether lovely
She was sitting, her soul looked out generously
She was sitting thinking of and only of Divinity
I looked and wondered who she was,
and the wind whispered Mary

She was sitting in a wave of clear consciousness
She was sitting just watching visions heavenly
She was sitting just reading the book of life
She was sitting radiating to all things this light
I looked and wondered who she was,
and the wind whispered Mary

She was sitting liberated from all things earthly
She was sitting and only absorbing bright light
She was sitting in the presence of truth eternal
She was sitting seeing only the sun of Suns
When I looked and wondered who she was,
and the wind whispered Mary

She was sitting in the body maiden
She was sitting in a land of freedom
She was sitting in a heavenly vibration
She was sitting in a pure light divine
I looked and wondered who she was,
and the wind whispered Mary

Although many poets and song writers are vague as to where the inspirations come from, let me be clear that this inspiration came directly to me from Meister Eckhart, a fourteenth century Dominican, mystic, writer, and teacher. He writes that "he of Sterngassen" was often asked what Our Lady was doing when the Angel appeared. He may have borrowed his inspiration too. Inspiration is good like that. Twenty-one things then were predicated to her and these things are a testimony to her exulted state. I translated that piece into a poem.

Be Silent Then Sing

If I were to sing a song just for you
I'm not entirely sure that I would be true
I might be seeking an invisible and unknown advantage
But if I were free to just focus upon me
Aligning the levels of my bodies and destiny
It's possible that crystal clarity might just re-emerge
No games to play in this silk interior
No rhythm or rhyme for my parched exterior
No tally of deeds that have been done
No promise of a life of love on the run
Just a giant mirror to reflect, a simple heart to inspect
Now, grown wings through this mind and sight
Into this sky of blue timeless light, a pulsing light beacons so bright
For eyes that are only just beginning, to see the space where eternity meets time
What parts to lose and what will survive
I behold my two eyes are turning back to One
Before me the light of one thousand suns
I pause before the awe that overwhelms me
Suddenly my effort has finished, as, sounds have slipped slowly into silence
I think I'll dive into this sea, the sea of eternity for a swim before returning, to
Sing.

Seeds to Sow

Your fate may wish to follow a foreseen and predictable road
But your destiny/mastery could free you another
A Blind Will will fall and fall upon the goal
For greater spirits, a blazed access avoids the trouble
If a face is formed in stone and doom
Nary a flower-sweet shall one summer watch bloom
One cannot hear the footsteps of the softly descending rain
If the sounds of past and future boom
Loosing the Eternal Nowness of things
Often left to trial again and again and again
And sitting behind clumsy and loud hastening hooves....
Looking up, one may see the ease of brighter days
Beacon lights wallowing on green velvet hills
Far oft voices have psalms to sing of heavenly praise
Seeds to sow, birds to sing and gentle wind to carry them
If only to align with a magnificent Will
A Will of wonder of knowledge and might
Fires eternal lit burning in a wide-open blaze
Shine a light on the lightness of things.
Lightness of being, lightness of seeing
lightness of feeling, of shape and of color and tone
Who knew of this hidden spirit's choice?
Who knew of the deep recessed voice?
Who first called for the flag to be raised?
When was this treasure first elevated and praised?
Who sent the morning light our way?
To loll and to ease our sense and place.
Anyway, who?

Let your own secret soul reveal this,
Let your own inner mind ascend to this,
Let it be your own beings decree a knowing and a bliss
To own and to live, to love and to learn, intuitively
From inside inspiration
To live, to love and to learn
intuitively

Light Leads Life

If the life you lead conceals the light that you are, you lose
When you walk, walk tall and let your soul guide your shoes
The soul of a man is greater than any fate
Remember Gandhi was thrown from a train
Still he was not at all troubled of being late
He arrived right on time at his destination of Freedom
and carried humanity upon his back

The day bringer walks through the night to his morning of victory
and glow
Bless the mountain that you are standing upon
and the wind and the rain and the snow
Walk softly and carry a big stick
Wearing a crown
of Suns and Stars
of Galaxies and Moon
Gaze inside your robe of experience
A little star dust you must sprinkle
on these hollowed grounds

Jump in and swim at the river of chance
Avoid the alligators of despair
Inside of you is a fountain of youth

Even as around you, all seems to be transitioning
Another cycle, another swim
Someone has turned on the moving lights again
Some say this is the greatest time to be alive
Now, is there really any other
Now, is there really any other

Cycles within cycles, wheels within wheels
Your SELF the point of stillness
It is all moving to thrill
From the cradle of your innocence and power
Comes forth a Sun
A life giving, life loving One
And wisdom can only flow from experience
and Love can only flow from your heart
and Power can only flow from the one source you know
the nameless One
The One some simply call great

Deep within you now, remember your ancestors
Deep within you remember your source
Deep within you, throw the switch
that lights the lights that lights
the lights that lights your torch

A glowing being is a liberated one
who calls forth electrons and protons
just for fun
To assemble his dream fired
fantasies and co creations
All to the glory of the One
Go,
Now!

Freedom Mirror

Freedom is a mirror that everyone can use
and if you can stand there straight and tall,
you must have paid your dues
The Buddha had a mirror and so much time he spent
He looked and stared and journeyed there
till all his karma went
Gandhi stood and gazed before he was put in jail
He went and shifted history, everybody knows the tale
When his men were hit, with bamboo sticks marching up salt hill
The results were so astonishing the whole of India was thrilled
Freedom
40 days and 40 nights, Jesus stared into it too
He placed that mirror in our hearts
So we could look, its true
When freedom calls you must not stall
To walk where skies are blue
The wisdom ones
Walk towards the Sun
In everything they do

Silent Again

Locah Samastah Sukino Bhavantu
Locah Samastah Sukino Bhavantu
Locah Samastah Sukino Bhavantu
Locah Samastah Sukino Bhavantu

I was reciting the prayer over and over

May the blessing flow
May all sentient beings be blessed
May I become an instrument of blessings for blessings sake.

When suddenly a silence fell upon my instrument

A sound arose and then a word

Suddenly my eyes opened, and I could hear the Sound with my Eyes

I had never heard a word with my eyes before

I wondered in awe if this could be true

Sure enough as soon as I closed my eyes everything went

Silent again

Try this now if you like
Open Eyes: Sound, Seeing, Om, Word

Closing Eyes: Silence

Open Eyes: Sound, Seeing, Om, Word

Closing Eyes: Silence

See, it's easy!

Close Eyes: Silence again!

See / No Karma / Eyes / I

One moment I look at the world and <u>say</u> there is no such thing as Karma.
Next moment I look at the world and <u>see</u> there is nothing out there but cause and effect.
It all depends on which world I am looking at.
Next moment I look at the world and <u>say</u> there is no such thing as Karma
One moment I look at the world and <u>see</u> there is nothing out there but cause and effect.
It all depends on which Eyes I am looking with.
There is Truth and there is truth.
Real Truth cannot be shaken, stolen or taken.
When your Eye is single your whole body will be full of Truth,
As Light.
The only trouble
is seeing double,
duality.
Eyes
See
I
See

I Believe

I believe in God
I believe in the Oneness of God
I believe in the Absolute Love of God
I believe in the God of my being
I believe in the God of all being
I believe in the God beyond our belief
I believe in the One God with all my being
I believe in the God beyond my being
I believe in the One God of Grace
I believe in the One God of All time and All space
I believe I AM grateful to exist in this place.
I believe for myself and for all sentient beings.
The holiness of the awareness of silent mindful breathing
Opens
And then
Emptiness

Is

The Key

I fashioned a key made of gold inlaid with precious stones,
diamond and opal
to open the door to the heavens,
I traveled through the secret fields of thought, of dreams,
of mountains, of streams,
of sacred sites, of craters and canyons, of temples, of cathedrals,
of halls, even Yee Sphinx had my footprints around her palm trees and
sandy base.
The pyramids I approached upon a mid-summer's eve,
for a fly-by, on a spirit winged driven glimpse,
floating, with a moon so full and so bright.
Now along this fleeting back rolling path
a ghost of myself, transient and vanishing,
called out loud to the gate keeper.
At last I have found the gate, I AM a key holder, please will you wait.
Subtle images of what I hoped would be streamed along
And flew past winged memories of what once seemed to be.
Paradise groves and peacock wings colored for love,
Bright rolling hills gave a color green a proud reason to be.
Blue mountains mapped a sun-cleared horizon of days,
A whisper of song on a passionate breeze of many-hued flames.
And call out I did, to the dawn, the dawn of all golden days.
At last I have found the gate, I AM a key holder, please will you wait.
I fashioned my feet to move so swift and so free,
My mind I thought was clear, as clear as clear could be.
And now I approached the towering temple of time,
Clutching joy, hope, possibility, and a direction safe, so sweet,
avoiding silent's vacant way, any sky of doubt or shadow.
At last I turned and stared into a bright light golden white
tunneling within.

A Sacred heart emerged with three bright burning flames
One pink, one golden, one blue.
What lay before me no man can say, no words can explain,
nowhere to begin.
A moment of Self redemption,
Arrives!
I called out loud to the gate keeper.
At last I have found the gate, I AM a key holder, please can you wait.
I looked and gazed down upon my melting hands, dripping carbon
turning crystalline.

There was no key to be seen, no bone, alone, just rainbow light there
seemed to be.
I saw the arch that was open and welcoming and warm,
And heard a voice calling out to me, softly.
I AM the Door no man can shut, no need for any key.
Come on in, Come on in, he gently called out to me
Come on in the Resurrection's free.
A sweet soft warm humbling voice called out again,
to this home bound hesitating me.
I AM the Door no man can shut
Come on in the Resurrection is free.

As our journey together now ends,
Your journey begins:

To Teach, to Train, to Inspire and to Illuminate

APPENDIX I
The Affirmations

The following affirmations define the intent and character of each of the Diamond Heart sessions. The energy for each session is a causal/etheric energy template that activates the individuals requesting the activation. It is, in essence, a baptism of Sacred Fire from the octave of love, the octave above. The discipline of spiritual unfolding is the directing of Intention, the receptivity of allowing and the appreciation for grace.

1. Body Elemental—Body Awareness—Alignment of the Trinity: I AM the resurrection and the life of my body/mind and spirit.
2. Communication: I AM multidimensional communications.
3. Guidance and Intuition: I AM being divinely guided.
4. Co-Creation, Talents, Productivity: I AM a magical being of infinite creativity.
5. Covenants, Purpose, Plan: I AM unfolding my covenants and unfolding the divine plan.
6. Organization and Co Operation: I AM re-defining, re-developing, and re-directing my personal database to be in alignment with my higher self.
7. Synergy and Fluidity: I AM up-regulating, up-grading automatically.
8. Self-Maintenance, Filtration & Protection: I Am a being of violet fire.
9. Grounded in Awareness: I AM the balance and harmony God desires on Earth right now.
10. Peace, Power and Prosperity: I AM manifesting all that I need, want, and desire.
11. I dream with Awareness and Recall: I AM awake in life, my dreams I recall.
12. The Returning Point, The Octave, Angel Eyes: I AM accessing my gifts developed in the past.

APPENDIX II
Declaration of the Light

I have the inner light and strength to forgive myself for every emotion of anger and fear that I have gone through this past day, week, year and back as far as I can reach,

I forgive myself and everyone who may have offended me.

I will let go and forgive the universe and all its people and conditions that have pushed me to the dark side of myself.

I forgive myself for giving up on people who deserved more from me, who deserved a second chance, with more compassion and understanding.

I forgive all that have cast zingers at my heart, my dreams, my ideas, and my soul.

Forgiveness is my healing balm, mentally I rub this on my heart and soul. Forgiveness is the tune I sing and the dance I move my feet to, also.

I forgive and become a living vortex of light and positive energy transforming myself through acceptance of what is. By accepting those people around me whom I have been challenged to understand fully, not knowing their unique place in God's unfolding universe.

I send this Statement of Forgiveness to the One and in return I am being set free, to be myself, liberated.

I shall not sweat the small stuff.

APPENDIX III

The Reset Exercise

Dear Anyone and/or Everyone,

If I have compromised you, or caused you harm, in any way possible, either for real or imagined, in this life or any other life, in this dimension or any other dimension, I humbly apologize to you. I ask for your complete forgiveness here and now.

And I forgive you likewise.

Also, I release myself from having to contribute to your wellbeing in all ways unless you specifically ask. I am here to work on myself!

And I release you likewise.

You are a great human being. We have the same Creator.

I AM perusing my destiny and completion with planet Earth and its fine people. *I AM* returning home, in LIGHT fashion.

You are completely excused from having to either understand or appreciate what this means to ME.

There is no assessment or validation that you must make about my decisions. You are free to move forward respectfully!

You may choose to ask God or not, what the plan for me is. I am in partnership with Her!

I am finished explaining myself! I am finished trying to explain myself!

I AM not a victim in any way shape or form. I accept responsibility for what I attract in my life; therefore, I reserve this right for myself and for you!

If I feel, intuit or observe in any way that you or any other person is compromised by blocks, blindness, cords, distortions, entities, karma, cooties, crap, time capsules, openings, spiral tracks, thought forms, trauma imprints, gas or any other condition: I reserve the right to head for the hills. I support OUR Freedom to Choose!

My moment of Now is Sacred and Self-sustaining. It has a future pull and so it does NOT require any traction from *any* past, whatever reality, idea, dream, or nightmare it may be.

I AM a heart centered being of Light on Purpose, *I AM* sending out a blessing to all life! Not because (state your name) is, was, or will continue to be, but simply because, *I AM*.

I AM here and now re-setting my goals, practice, and orientation for ALL my relationships. All cords are cut and, only heartstrings need apply

Namáste!

APPENDIX IV
Re-Set / Namáste Exercise

After reading the Re-Set Exercise out loud the *Namáste* greeting brings more emotion to the surface, tears of joy and laughter of release.

We have experimented with going around the room and having each person who wishes to, to read a sentence of the Re-Set out loud. This charges the room with a larger than individual intent and promotes a group chemistry.

Namáste is a greeting from heart to heart.
Namáste is the recognition that God stuff abides here.
Namáste transcends the flesh to the Spirit of Fellowship and
the Heart of Belonging.
Namáste is this flow of a finer wave of the lightness of Being.

Let each person who is present and who cares to participate, simply move around the room and do the *Namáste*, hands across the heart, blessing for one another.

Allow enough time for each person to *Namáste* all they like.

Allow time for integration.

Namáste

APPENDIX V

Bija Seeds ☼ Mantra Meditation
Free Gifts of Light/Sound/Energy
A Heart Mantra for you

Thousands of years ago and before the written language was the repository for the richness of cultures, holy men, sages, and wise men and women were always present within all groups of people. We find similarities of traditions such as with the Huna of Hawaii and tribes in Africa. People existing who had no contact with one another but who developed ideas, philosophy and names for things that were identical. The subconscious mind and its discoveries, generally attributed to Freud and Jung, were understood, and appreciated by the early Shamans of many cultures.

The very rich traditions of India that gave birth to the beings like Buddha, Padmasambhava (who brought Buddhism from Tibet to India) and Shankara (founder of Vedanta) offer us insights into the nature of man as an evolving spiritual being, a diamond in the rough but still capable of unfolding the wonders and perfections of a Christ. Solving the riddle of the Sphinx, like discovering the Philosopher's Stone or finding the kingdom within, is the last great mystery for man to solve. Science can put a man in space, but can we discover the space within a man that resonates with the highest ideas, ideals, unity, divinity, Self and Source or God?

This was, is and will always be sole purpose of the initiate who brings the Sacred Science of Nam, or the Word, or the Mantra to the ears of the disciple of truth, to push back the barriers to self-knowledge and discover what was always already the case. God and Man are One. Bija Seeds are gifts from the Creator filled with etheric energy to fuel one's own personal journey inward toward light, freedom, creativity, wisdom, the sacred, the Source or God. Bija is the seed sound and energy that proceeds all form. Mantras are powerful vibrations that work at the atomic level to assist human beings in the journey of being and becoming, of awakening.

The Mantra, the OM or Amen is beyond religion and/or perhaps before it. The Seed resonates with your primordial self and aligns one's body/mind/spirit with the cause of its existence, delivering empowerments of knowledge, sensitivity, virtue, and proofs of our eternal connection with one another and with the Supreme Being, Supreme Intelligence, the Omnipotent, present Omniscient One, in a most rewarding, step by step unfolding and glorious fashion.

A more complete study of the meditation process can be found in Section Two, page

22, in the *Life Seed Documents* found at LifeSeedCodes.com.

This GIFT, although valued in meditation centers for thousands of dollars, is offered as a free gift of love and light at most Life Seed and Diamond Heart events. Receive a gift that keeps on giving. Let your keen focus resonate a complete and wholesome path of fulfillment, satisfaction, and wonder; become more heart centered.

APPENDIX VI
What Diamond Heart Energy Activations *are NOT*

What is clear to me after the practice of energy work and meditation for many years is that one is constantly in a more focused state of self-discovery and creativity. It is important in considering participating in the research and guided meditations that one understands what these activations are NOT.

1. This is not a form of therapy, or hypnosis of any kind or persuasion.
2. This is not a religious belief program.
3. This is not the practice of medicine, diagnosis, or mental health assessment.
4. There are no beliefs required outside a normal trust that one is connected to a universal power that created us and maintains us, and that we are connected to this source of power through grace. Your sovereignty is held as a sacred trust.
5. Participants are free to stop this inquiry at any time either during the session or after any session. Participation is totally voluntary. Each session is scheduled as desired.
6. There are NO suggestions or advice given concerning one's way of living, one's relationships and affiliations in any way that may be considered directives.
7. There is never any recruiting to join any organization, group, or congregation.

The Gifts

Who we are is a gift from the Creator. That we are is the gift from the Creator. What we do with the gift is our gift back to the Creator and the creation. The fact that you can work on yourself, improve yourself and continue in your evolution is the creator's continual gift to you.

The work we do to resurrect, redeem, and renew oneself is our gift back to the creation. You can believe in a higher power (that which is buried within you) to assist you, to inspire you, to unfold you. If you are waiting for someone else to come along and do the work for you, well some believe that you may be in for a rude awakening, which may be good anyway. There may be an easier way to go about the business of being and becoming. The life seed codes presented in this book are powerful introductions to ideas, strategies and wholesome wellness seeds and practices that may assist you on a more powerful climb on the mountain of self.

It is our greatest wish for you arrive alive in that constant stream of renewal and to be blessed in all way and always, it is that simple. Some say that the "now" of eternity is always fresh and all ways new. You cannot step into the same stream twice. Together we can focus a strong attitude of openness, readiness, and redemption. Together let us take the next step.

From the publishers, writers, editors, and contributors we wish you and bless you in the light off discovery, all the best. You are That.

I AM Workbook Diamond Heart Energy Activations
Be Clear Now!
Life Seeds and Codes

Thank you for purchasing the Life Seeds and Codes book.

The synergy of these three method books is important in appreciating strategies for the Body, Mind and Spirit. My journey with clearing and pendulum work began over forty years ago. That is why I am offering to you, the access, to the purchaser of Life Seeds and Codes, the charts and meditations. The dowsing charts in the book *Be Clear Now* and all 12 guided meditations on the *Diamond Heart Energy Activations* are available to you as my gift.

Just send an email to me at brianrobertsbodywork@gmail.com requesting this and I will send you the files for the charts and the access to the 12 guided meditations through Drop Box.

In Service to the One,

Brian T Roberts

Go to http://Lifeseedcodes.com for updates on the Brain Body Balancing method.

ABOUT THE AUTHOR

Rev. Brian T Roberts

I have been trying to remain as anonymous as possible here in the process of releasing the Diamond Heart Energy Activations. I became a massage therapist in 1976 and at a seminar I was taking years later our instructor told us to learn to meditate because we would be working on a lot of sick people and would need to "stay clear." I got involved with Hakomi work, a form of Body Centered Psychotherapy for a few years doing training in this work.

I came from a harsh background and took a significant amount of physical abuse growing up. All of the systems of mind-body-spirit integration that I explored professionally were first and foremost for myself, for my own healing. I had incredible teachers and really kept after it for many years. I graduated from the seminary of the Church of Ageless Wisdom and was exposed to great teachings and amazing people.

I was a movement enthusiast and studied and taught the Flomotion movement awareness system for four years. I trained in a system of Hypnotherapy for one year and received sessions weekly. It took me about twenty years to ground myself in meditation. Nowadays there are many more support systems to help us. In the process of trying to find the right meditation teacher and system, I encountered many Yogi's, Christian mystics, Buddhist Lamas, Hakomi folk, Sufi's, channels, mediums, Transcendental Meditation instructors, dowsers, and many current day quantum energy systems people. All of it was and is a part of my knowledge and experience base. I practiced Alpha Brain Body balancing for ten years and during that time I performed weddings, christenings, and meditation initiations. For many years I woke up at 4 a.m. to meditate. I cannot do this right now because I need to be more active in the world.

I truly wish I could have shared all these things with friends and family. Perhaps some will join me in this trio of teachings.

Falling/Rising into a relationship with our True Self or "I AM" demands that we follow our hearts. *Be As You Are* because you are a star. Be inspired by everyone you can be inspired by. Kahil Gibran said in the book *The Prophet* to never put your heart into anyone's hands for only the hand of life can contain your heart. I personally left a lot of gurus because they all had their own agendas.

Listen to the sound of the mantras and read the poems and meditations in the book and you will know enough about the author. My work with organizing the CD's and the books is done. Now I AM starting a new journey to meet my Self in all the Selves I meet on the journey, in light and mutual respect. We are here to learn the lesson of togetherness.

Let's get it done.

Namáste
Brian T Roberts
Minister of Light and Sound